The Woma

By
Sheldene D. Byron

Revised Edition
Foreword By Dr. Julian S. Ferdinand

Cover Design: Pro Art Design One

Contact info:
Email: AmbSDByron@outlook.com
WhatsApp- (1-868) 729-7876
Facebook- https:/www.facebook.com/sheldene.byron

Dedication

 This book is wholeheartedly and affectionately dedicated to a woman whose heart and labour of love, sacrifice and selflessness merited a rare volume of grace and faith to me - My beloved mother, Venita Z. Byron. The magnitude of her strength, faith and impeccable ambition, though not recognized on the wall of fame, has left an indelible mark in my life, one that cannot be denied. Mother, for this, I say *'Thank you'*. Truly, you lived to see the difference and transformation that the cross made possible in and through me. (Rest In Eternal Peace: Sunrise 28th March 1948, Sunset 15th November 2009)

To all the women whom God has allowed to touch my life significantly and to bring me to a place of recognizing the astounding beauty possessed deep within the wealth of my soul. Women whom I call, *"Midwives"* and would truly express gratitude to, for opening their hearts and lives to me. Words cannot express the volume of grace I found in all of you. From my heart I simply say, *'thank you'*. God surely used you beyond measure to help me see the worth and value of my femininity, and the excellence of His creation as a woman. I love you!!

Foreword

Do not consider it strange that the foreword to *"The Woman in Me"* is being written by a man. This provides ample evidence that the thoughts captured in this book, although focused on women, go beyond the gender barriers, biases and embraces all people. It is considered good reading for both genders, all age groups, and for people of all cultures.

Throughout this book, the writer, Sheldene D. Byron, constantly invites readers to seek a closer relationship with God. She regularly invites the readers to *"look in the mirror"* and to engage in the introspection and self-analysis that provides the foundation for those who will be proactive in seeking that closer walk with God. She is convinced, and so am I, that the women who read this book and accept the challenge to better their best efforts will become more Kingdom-focused and be better mothers, wives, sisters, co-workers, neighbours, and friends.

Sheldene shares some very personal childhood and adolescence experiences and explains how these shattered her innocence and so many of her childhood dreams. She vividly recalls the traumatic experiences. The reader has no choice but to empathize with her and other vulnerable individuals who have gone through or may be going through similar experiences. Her personal revelations confirm that deviant behaviours can create and sustain feelings of low self-worth. But she does not record these traumatic situations in search of the reader's pity or sympathy. It is quite evident that these experiences are shared as testimony that broken individuals (especially vulnerable females) can rebuild their lives and find purpose and victory in living a God-centered life.

Ms. Byron's book emphasizes the need for young persons to have good role models and mentors – especially during the vulnerable stages of their lives. She is a skillful story-teller who uses her experiences to invite readers to seek to play a more active role in intercepting those persons who are likely to be vulnerable to the circumstances that will imprison them with guilt and shame. However, she simultaneously invites those who may have fallen prey to such spiritually and emotionally decapitating experiences to break free with God's help and the importance of nurturing a God-centered life.

This book is excellent reading for persons who are seeking a closer walk with the Lord. It is also considered good reading for those who are engaged in counseling, coaching and mentoring others; especially those who may have been traumatized during their early childhood. Readers are likely to discover that as they read the final pages of this book they automatically wonder when Sheldene will produce the sequel to this timely literary work.

Dr. Julian S. Ferdinand
Visiting Lecturer
Arthur Lok Jack Graduate School of Business
Trinidad & Tobago W.I

Acknowledgement

Assuredly, God is my utmost source of inspiration and His wisdom truly reflects my heart and devotion in this book. Therefore, my sincere appreciation is extended to the following;

Dr. Edward Cumberbatch - Your words truly revealed that the pages penned were worth taking that step forward in faith. Thank you for igniting the flame and for being the first English lecturer to show me the gift of writing. (RIH)

Dr. Julian Ferdinand - Your articles provided a scope that widened my horizon and I am glad I took the courage to make contact with you. You have really encouraged and built my world of hope.

Ms. Kathleen Davis - You are such a blessing and a motherly gift, even in correcting and guiding me through the grammatical steps of making a good product. I am truly blessed to have had such a fulfilling experience with you, personally. I love the crystal in your tone. Thank you!

Mrs. Sherma Carter - The part you played, not just as a friend, but a mother in Zion who ensured I kept focused on the Call and Destiny within. You are a treasure for a lifetime Momz. Thank you for being my rock and confident. Now, you're able to see the *"God- Difference"*.

Mr. Jeffrey Byron - You're the first donor to something that only God intended to prove beyond words and I'm glad you stayed as a covenanter to my life, especially in prayer and as a *'Father'*. Thank you!

Se Jilla Mc Dowall - If there is one word I can fit here to describe or authenticate the blessing you have been in my life, I would simply say, *"Faithful".* Our friendship and love opened our hearts in ways that God knew would have brought about such a seed of legacy in the earth. Thank you for standing and supporting me in this humble regard. Love you Cous!

Apostle Sherell Shelby- You're a phenomenal gift and an exceptional model of my heart. Thank you for the extra push and love to see the call on my life reach beyond the limits of my own abilities. I am honored to do life with you!!

Dr. Lovella Mogere- My mentor, agitator, confident and greatest *THRUSTER*, you made me pick up my pen again. You saw what I couldn't see and now, here I am reediting this fine product, because you believed in my *INK*. My love and honor for you goes above the norm. Thank you!!

My Siblings - Although we're in different places and spaces, I'm glad we can share in this experience and I do hope that the pages in this book would reignite and stir your hearts to believe that what God has done in me, surely He can do in each of you. Our Mother lived, now let us live by the exemplary faith she has set and let's dare to *BUILD* a greater legacy for the next generation. From my heart, to yours.

TABLE OF CONTENTS

☐

A Note from the Author

I cannot begin to tell you how much my heart aches to see women today, living below their spiritual aptitude, altitude and failing to understand innately their *'God-given'* nature and purposes on earth. Although I have had my share of shakes in life, in order to find this worthy essence of living through Jesus Christ, I firmly believe each woman on earth can aspire to a state of fulfillment and be in the ideal of a *New Creation*. No doubt about it!

We have gone too far from what Eden's identity ignited in us at creation's door. We are more comfortable with fighting for our own *'Rules And Rights'* while forfeiting the excellence of our worth and grace. We have even allowed certain practices and traits from our culture and tradition to keep us captive from exercising our full potential as God's divine instruments. Too many of us have been wounded and left to revive on our own and society has cheapened our livelihood into what is professed to be the *'nowadays'* supermodel for women.

Women, can we please stop for a minute, breathe, and simply look at what we're up against. It's not about a man's world as we've been taught and neither is it vice versa. It's about understanding our functions and learning to combine each one as God directed in the beginning. Can we go back and find out where we've lost it? Can we uncap the fountain that has caused so much chaos and bring ourselves back onto the path that will lead us into realizing the gift God has given to our world? Can we simply be women, without the fussing, fighting, shouting, screaming and all the emotional tones that have created an imbalance within our construction and design as women? Can we talk straight for once and come to terms with our own errors?

For too long we've been battling. I believe this is an aligned specimen to *TIME,* that God is ushering to bring us back into divine order so that our lives can become the product He designed us to be, and in this, we will live victoriously. Will you allow Him to unmask all that's within you to bring you back to basics, to a place where your worth, value and beauty can shine beyond your imagination? Are you willing to let God erase everything to open your eyes to see His reflection on the inside of you and the womanhood He's created for you to enjoy in full? Why not give yourself the chance to see His hands come alive through your femininity? Why not let your life take the shape that He's always desired for you to embrace in full?

Walk with me through this book and you will be guided towards seeing your life anew through God's eyes. You'll be able to see the magnitude of essence He has for you to inherit, and the volume of grace to bring you into the woman He has called you to be on earth. Women, God is calling us back to Eden- Our birthplace, Our foundation, Our home, and surely, Our destiny. Let's arise, let's take a stand together to become women in whom God would delight and cause to affect this world with all He has bestowed on us... Journey with me and let's dare to be *Kingdom Women- A New Creation In Christ!!*

Author
Sheldene D. Byron

Chapter 1

'The Genesis Effect'

"I'm quite amazed at the sight of how we as women are viewed by our world and despite the various attempts to correct or to bring light to these needed issues, many have failed to truly understand where we need to begin anew."

Ladies! Can we stop for a minute, pause and take a good look at where we are in life today? Can I humbly suggest that you take a seat in a comfortable chair or sofa that suits your liking and let's have a sensible chat? Let's take a closer look at our state as women, in our homes, churches, workplaces and other environs. Can we examine our context as women from a new perspective and come to terms with who we truly are and can become? Although the world has painted its picture about us, I believe many of us are still trying to grapple with our image, identity and even our status as women; so much so that we have accepted the norms and traditions that are proposed by our cultures rather than applying God's initial context.

I'm quite amazed at the sight of how we as women are viewed by our world and despite the various attempts to correct or to bring light to these needed issues, many have failed to truly understand where we need to begin anew. And I must admit that it does not begin from the wisdom of man or the very ideals that cultivate our cultures and various forms of knowledge. It simply starts from within the mind of God, from *Genesis- The Beginning Of Creation*. For too long we've missed the mark as to who we are and can become and I am moved deeply to bring us back; to that place where we can learn effectively how to be

Kingdom women *(women who understand their 'God-given' nature and who would live in that nature as God desires)* and not just cultured women. Therefore, I am conscious of not just the need for us as women to understand who we are but more so that we come to the realization that we are far more than just what the world dictates and describes us to be. To be honest it's quite appalling to see the comparison between what the world thinks of us as women and how God thinks of us as women. And for some reason my mind often wonders why there is such a cheapening of women in society. Not that all can be qualified as cheap women in the same manner but it's overbearing to see just how much we've been taken for granted on so many levels.

Of course there are situations that would be accredited to decision making on the part of some of us women. And I am not going to ignore the fact that we're responsible for where we are and who we've become. Nonetheless, I am sensing the need for order and restoration from the Genesis context and if we are honest with ourselves we will admit that we've failed miserably. Just one look at the world and we will hang our heads in shame, wondering, where did we go wrong in the first place. So let's sit together and start afresh and see with God's eyes what we've been missing and see how best we can appropriate God's standard in our lives as women.

Recently, at a Vision's Conference, I was corrected by one of the presenter's about the way we teach the Bible. For years we have been starting from mid-way of the book and not from the beginning- *Genesis*. This is so true! Think of it, when we get a new believer or convert, do we start from the book of Genesis or from the book of St. John? If we're honest, we will say St. John, because that's what we've all been taught and so we pass it on. But the truth is we need to start at the beginning, lest we teach only half of the book and not the whole, which means that we would be sharing only part of the Bible and not the whole Bible. So with that little thought, let's start at the beginning where all things from God came into being and were ordered into creation.

Genesis- New Beginnings, has always stirred my mind especially as to how God created by just speaking. I find it quite fascinating that God would just speak and things suddenly appear from nowhere. Wow! And I would really wish I could do that but the truth is, *"I Can!"*. If we take into context God as Creator of the universe and we (*the human race*), the created, who inhabit the universe, then we would recognize that we are recipients of the Creator's nature. We are made in His image and likeness *(Gen.1:26-28),* therefore we have the capacity, the creative ability; to generate that which is more than able to produce what we speak into being. Yet many hardly take the time to understand this crucial sense of wisdom and fail to capitalize on its potent foundation.

God in all that He is, detailed creation in such a manifold way by causing one of the best conceptions to be derived from His intuition. He simply *Thought, Spoke* and then **'Man'** came into being. This aspect of creation is so important to God. With great admiration and meaning for His creation, He provided every necessity for man so that he can be welcomed into his new environment. Man had no void, absolutely nothing was missing. In the very nature of man, the knowledge that he was created with every possible ability to create on his own was not exempted. To fully compliment his creation, God brought him *(Man)* a help meet suitable for him, one of his kind, equal to his nature, one who is a compatible companion, one who would add virtue and value to his life. *(Gen.1:20-25)*

Now, Eden was in full effect and the Creator admired His handiwork. God had done something exceptional, so phenomenal that He thought that the best thing to do was to bring His final creation to man and he called her **'Woman'.** The funny thing is, God was the one who came to the realization that the man's complete needs must be met. He did not decide to cheat man out of anything since He was the one who caused the dust to form man and breathed into him so that he became a living entity of creation. God knew after everything He had created, Eden in full, that man could not be exempted from the fullness of His wonders. After all, everything of its kind was already made and man had worked hard enough to finalize his order in the garden. Thereafter, it was absolutely necessary for God to conclude man's need.

Moreover, God had to complete His thoughts and design of creation in full, so nothing could be without form. Each need to Him was crucial and He knew in His wisdom that His last creation would seal the deal entirely. This is the reason why nothing was missing from creation, absolutely nothing! In Him everything was made and by Him all things were made. This was His perfect order, creation was His own and in as much as He knew that, God allowed for freedom to be a part of man's destiny. Wow! I wish we can get back to Eden and live in its wonder. Oh! How we've missed the mark so bad.

So how are we going to face the music before us, knowing that we're far from what creation reveals to us from Genesis? How are we going to get back to basics and come to terms with our errors because we are so distant from our original design that God has so wisely created? Notice, when Adam and Eve were created, they dwelled independently, individually, and yet collectively as *ONE*. Their entire scope of humanity was holistic, not partial, creation was a part of them and they knew their entire lives were instinctively centered on the Creator. Eden was their habitat but God was their life-spring, their gene effect, their absolute and most dependable source. This was the Genesis of God's marvelous conception and He did it to effect His own thoughts and words, so that creation can experience His benevolence.

So ladies! Where have we gone wrong and how were we able to drift so far from Eden? How come we lost so great a glimpse of God's order and design? Is it impossible to get back to basics, to start over and strive to become what God has always intended? Absolutely not! This is the ultimate context that God desires for us to become a part of. And by no means is it unachievable or unattainable, except, if we deceive our own mindsets into thinking that this is beyond you or me. Surely God has not changed His perspective of Eden; so why should we change our perspective as His creation. I believe what we mostly struggle with is the effect of Genesis chapter 3- the fall of man and how we have been deceived by the enemy in the game of life.

Let's not be too quick to jump and say, *"It was the woman's fault, not the man."* I can imagine the horns sounding and the shouts of the men, Amen, Amen! And if we are thinking in this way we have already missed the mark. Remember, this is not an issue for the *'Blame-Game'.* It is simply trying to help us come to terms with the deficiency and to see how we can re-gene our nature back to Eden and live accordingly.

Therefore, we need to come to the understanding that God is willing to work with us wherever we are in our walk of life, no matter the conditions, situations, circumstances and the image that we project at present. Nothing is impossible with God *(Mark 9:23)*. Yes, we have fallen from Genesis but it is not impractical for us to raise the bar afresh and start anew to recapture what we've missed in the beginning. I am challenging us as women to seriously lift our standards and start seeing ourselves as God sees us.

We have left our image of Eden and swallowed what the world has thrown out to us and I believe this is the time and season that God is calling us back to Eden. So let's raise our flags and start marching; because the world is still awaiting the *'Genesis-Women'* to take form and become all that God has called us to be. Let's go forward with God, knowing that He is the designer's original and can make us affect the earth with His wonder.

Chapter 2

'Face The Mirror'

We are God's creation and all in all we must face His truth regardless of how we feel, think or wish to divert from the reality of His order of life. We've heard it said, over and over, "No man is an island, self contained."

When last have you looked or observed your image in the mirror? Yes You! I think it's a fair and simple question. Hmmm! Some of you may be wondering why I am asking such a question. But from a realistic point of view, if you can't tell, perhaps, you should try it right now! Come on; get up off the comfy seat for a minute or two. Go on, take a good long, hard look at yourself! Face You! If time does not permit at this moment, then make a conscious effort to do it at some point, maybe right after you finish dressing for an occasion or when you're heading off to a shower; or after getting ready for work. Just take some time to look at you. I mean really take in you for yourself. If possible, do so when no one else is around. Actually, I'm extending this invitation because I just need you to see yourself up close and be personal for a good minute or two. I'm not talking about one of those flash moments where you just take a glimpse and move on. No honey! I'm asking you to seriously stop, and take a good look at you, for once in your life. Just look at you!

What do you really see? I guess you never really stopped to see or much less admire your uniqueness as a woman. And to be honest, it's an inviting pleasure to absorb your entire image, face to face. So I am imploring you to go ahead and take a good look. Yes, look at you, in all your fullness as a woman, God's creation. It won't hurt to look! The actuality is when you can see yourself in such a reflective way, it often shows up the true *"YOU"* that person you seldom see, may have never faced or confronted. This is where the mask is revealed, that part of you that has been hidden for so long, that part that you've tucked away in a cocoon, afraid to even let the sunlight shine on it. But the truth is, if you cannot face '*You*' the likely-hood is that you will run from yourself for a very long time. So it's time for you to stop running and face '*You*'!

For Genesis to take its course of activation in our lives, one thing that we will have to confront constantly is **'Truth'**. And there is really no reason for us to continue running from what we need to bring attention to in our lives. As I said before, we have all fallen. The human race has suffered tremendously, and our state of defect needs to be addressed. This is not about pointing fingers. We've done that for too long and the longer we waste time on such trivial matters, the longer the enemy will keep us from progressing to Eden. My simple reason for stating this is, that is the exact place where we tend to miss the mark. And the enemy will do anything to block our efforts to attain or even recapture the scope of Eden in our lives. No wonder he scored on us big time from that very habitation. No wonder his deceptions were filled with such atrocious poison, that we were so mixed up in such a frenzied game that we hardly took time to see the horror of his aim in the beginning *(Gen. 3:1-7)*.

Yet we go on every day trying to still fix things in our lives when the damage has already taken full effect. We were played and we were scored upon, that's the truth. Yes! I say **'We'** without hesitation. Both male and female were outsmarted, conned, trapped, fooled, tricked, out

[19]

mastered, name it, we fell for the bait and lost the game. So there is no need for us to fool ourselves into thinking that we need to pass or cast blame. In fact, Adam and Eve were stopped in their tracks for such outrageous behavior *(Gen. 3:8-11).* So tell me, what is all the blah, blah, blah about the *'Blame-Game'* issue? Does it really make sense for us to fight with each other, when we are responsible for our actions? I think not!

My grace filled ladies, let's try our best to realign ourselves with the perspective of Eden and face the mirror with a sense of dignity and truth. There is no need for shouting and raging war. Work with me here! Take off the defense mechanism. Take off the gloves! And yes! Take off everything that you may wish to pelt at me and the men. Listen, we've fought long enough, for decades and centuries. And we need to pull the plug at once, check ourselves in the mirror and examine our hearts before God.

Our fallen state is what needs to be addressed. It does not make any sense for me to tell you that it is not affecting the globe. Just take a good look! The very human race is confused, frustrated and very little is being done to generate change in the way we think, perceive and live. You may say, "So what about the churches, and those who are trying to live the Christian way, doesn't that count for something?" While I would agree to some extent, unfortunately, we have not done all that we could and there is much more to be done with so little time.

Shall we face the mirror for ourselves and see how best we can convert our hearts to Eden? Now, my reason for addressing us as women, has more to do with the wealth of our creative design and the context of our image in God rather than what the world proposed. Simply expressed, we've lost sight of being **'WHOLE'** women. I've come to this conclusion because I've observed just how much we've missed the mark in fully representing God on earth. I'm stunned by the many women who only see themselves in the eyes of what man proposed. And fail to understand that God is the creator, the One, who made us for His own good pleasure. It hurts me to see women living as if they're just material for men. Women who limit their God given potential, who underestimate their worth and value in God. Women who for one reason or the other fail to capitalize on their gifts, abilities, potential and creativity. Women who misunderstand their functions in family life. Women who have not captured their vision and purpose on earth and the list goes on and on.

We have become adaptive to all sorts of agendas and have forfeited God's agenda. So much so that we are now wrestling to bring back some sort of image to ourselves in this 21st century. What a tragedy for the eons of years wasted. WOW! I think something should have hit us right in our faces, at this point, right here. Can we not face the mirror of truth? I'll ask the question again, "Where did we lose it?" Hmmm! Ladies I am troubled for us and I will admit that it pains me to see how we've been deceived and robbed. We have been imprisoned far too long, and I believe God's heart is yearning for the day when we will get a grip on our senses and redirect our lives according to His kingdom on earth. Then and there we will realize how much Eden is worth.

The whole world is crying for women to rise up to be better mothers, wives, parents, teachers, nurses, doctors, ministers, social activists, accountants, engineers, scientist, prayer warriors, champions, missionaries, principals, heads of government, better officials at work, models, singers, musicians, scholars, trained professionals and so much more. Although many women have risen to these positions, there is something that is still missing. The noise is still in the background and murmurings are still being heard. Why can't we work together to build our nations, societies, families, homes and the world at large? Is it so hard to achieve? Was God misled when He created us equal and desired for us to be one and function as a unit? I doubt it with all my heart.

Are we afraid to become Kingdom focused women or are we afraid of what the world would see us become through God's eyes? Let me reinforce a crucial point here ladies, our creation was never on account of man nor was our creation limited to any spectrum of inferiority. We were created for purpose driven reasons that God Himself ordained, not to be controlled by the world's standards or idealism. In the context of God's creation we are *'WHOLE'* beings. We are not subject to man's opinions and values. The truth is, God made us to be a helper or help meet to man, so we are not in any way limited to man's idea, for us to function fully as women. Lest we misunderstand our creative abilities and God's original perception of us as women.

In relation to the fall of man, we have so succumbed to failure that our minds bear the very imprint of what society expects of us. This is why we limit our role and functions to what the norm of traditions, customs and cultures ascribed. However, in as much as this is true, let's still be mindful that this is not an avenue for us to rise up against men and feel that we have the independence to run off and be women without the need of men. Even though we are independent women in our own right, it is not God's intention for us to work alone without needing each other.

Be very careful to note that this is not a revolutionary weapon to create more chaos but rather a conscious awareness of our fall as well as how we've been deceived in our thinking as opposed to how God sees us and desires for us to live. Eve is enough of an example for us to grasp the reality of our mistake, if we are thinking that way *(Gen. 3)*.

The truth is, the mirror clearly reflects both our nature and our hidden mask, the one with which we love to clothe ourselves and feel so comfortable in that there is no desire to change or even move from such a position. The mirror shows us exactly who we are, with all the added embellishments and personification of our well-decorated selves. However, when we step away from the mirror, we deceive ourselves into thinking that our image is left right in front of the said mirror but forget that it is projected wherever we go.

Why do we try so hard to cover ourselves from the light of truth? I have no idea! But is it not the truth that sets us free, eventually? Then, there is no real reason for us to turn our eyes and ears from the truth, especially when it's directed at our own hearts and faces. All we have to do is, be honest and face the mirror, that moment of reality which hinges on us coming to grips with the essence of what is eating away our world, way down on the inside of our souls and deal with it, not run from it.

We are God's creation and all in all we must face His truth regardless of how we feel, think or wish to divert from the reality of His order of life. We've heard it said, over and over, *"No man is an island, self contained."* In essence, no one person can survive without help from another, because man was not wired to operate separate and apart from woman. They're a unit with a unique *"Oneness-Oriented Mission"*, and that's the fundamental concept that originally started us to live in Eden, not *Inferiority-versus-Superiority, Headship versus Slavery,* and *Dominance-versus-Usurpy.* We will never achieve anything that pertains to God's desires, if we live like that. It would only ruin God's initial plan of creation. Instead, we need to start functioning from the *Genesis Model* if we're ever going to live successfully as God intended of us.

At this point, I would like to take us into some practical insights so that we can comprehend not just our fall, but the basis of Eden's need for realignment in our world as men and women. Now ladies, let's not get ahead of ourselves and forget that our image is what God's heart is towards our reflection of his design and intentions, not what we deem to be right in our own eyes. Remember we are aspiring towards God's original plan, that of Eden- *A Kingdom Perspective*- and bringing our creation to work out the plans of God in our lives. Therefore, let's go back to basics for a bit, and move forward to this aspect of becoming *'WHOLE'* women unto God.

Let's view how the mirror can unplug from within those areas that have been buried for so long. Those elements that we hardly ever wish to discuss and deal with, that have clogged up our lives from being fruitful and operative as women. Take this journey with me, and face the mirror on your own, even as I have done. And see how much you've missed in the whole process of living out your full aptitude as a woman. Let's get down to *brass-tacks* about the real issue before us. This may be a journey of harsh reality, or even one of redefinition, but the wholeness of creation is what I desire for you to attain and not just what is proposed by the world's concepts and ideals.

[24]

Therefore, let's face the mirror together, and begin anew to see how God can affect our lives with insights from Eden, and to become citizens of Eden in this time and season.

Chapter 3

'The Reflection In The Mirror'

In spite of what the world may think, what people may say, no one knows who you are going to be and what you are going to become until God reveals His image in you through the reflection of His Son in you.

As women, and when I speak of the term *'Women'* I am referring to all women in general, regardless of class, colour, status, creed or race. There is no barrier or distinction in this dialogue. For this reason, I am convinced that all of us have at some point faced uncertainties which we hardly share with any other person. Regrettably, this often bears marks of a past we seldom wish to unveil. Therefore, depending on the nature of such a past, it is imperative for us to realize that it will remain with us until we decide within ourselves that we need to deal with it. In fact, the truth to this can be expressed in this way, we cannot correct what we are not willing to confront, because it is in the correcting that change comes. At this point, when you face the mirror and you are reminded of your past you may not like what you see. On the contrary, there are those who will be content or believe that they are. Nevertheless, let's face the reality and acknowledge that's who we are, or permit me to say that this is how we would have allowed circumstances or situations to create the environment in which we are now living.

However, all is not lost. It's ok to feel that way when we look at ourselves. No harm done! But the real challenge comes when we realize that we are not comfortable with what we see, who we have turned out to be or what we've actually become. The question is, "What do you do when you find yourself in such an uncomfortable or awkward position?" Search yourself carefully. "Do you wish to be different?" "Or do you look at yourself in disgust, shame or perhaps wonder why or how you have come to this point in your life?" This is one question that shattered me at first when I truly began to face my own music, but I didn't allow it to detour my desire for change. Perhaps there are many questions lingering in your mind when you see your own reflection in the mirror. Yet there are those who will look and say, "Yes! I am fine, I feel good about myself or I am rather happy with what I've turned out to be." Some may even look and say, "Well, well am I not a beauty to behold."

Even though it's an exciting feeling to be able to recognize such things about yourself, I want to assure you that it's all alright to do so. At this point, I am not taking the path to address those who are well esteemed in such a position. But rather those who are tired of seeing themselves one way, and are just down right tired and sick of it all. Yes, I am here to encourage you to take a bold step forward, go ahead and look in that mirror. Look! You may not feel pleased or you may feel somewhat ashamed, disgusted, bitter, despicable and may even hate to admit it to yourself but that's alright. The truth is you are looking and that's the beginning.

Simply stand there and take a good, long, hard look at yourself. It's ok to face '*YOU.*' Perhaps all the memories of past pains, errors, failures, mistakes, disappointments or grievous occasions may come like a flowing river, streaming down like an uncontrollable current, wishing to find the end of the sea, just to attain freedom. Yes you will feel uneasy and you may not want to face up to the real '*YOU*' but I have news for you. I am

[27]

here to let you know that's a subtotal of who you are and not the complete '*YOU.*'

You may say, "Why me?" And, "Why did this have to happen?" Especially, if you have fallen into the trap of sexual abuse, incest, fornication, homosexuality, molestation, jealousy, adultery, lust, thief, physical and emotional abuse, prostitution, lesbianism, rape, attempted suicide, or bad relationships, name it. These issues are often the hardest to combat particularly, when you look in the mirror and that is all you can see. Simply because the pain and hurt are there circulating night and day in your mind. It becomes so unpleasant and disturbing that the very pit of your stomach wants to crawl and find a hiding place.

Honey, trust me. It hurts down to the core!!! And it makes no sense for me to tell you it doesn't. As a matter of fact, it's ok to feel hurt and to express your emotions rather than to kindle or nurse them until a later period. That's where real trouble begins!! You may ask, why? But the truth is, it becomes harder to deal with, since you would have found some sort of antidote to survive rather than taking the initiative to deal with them outrightly. Mind you, it's easy to convince yourself with the thought which may cause you to say to yourself, "I have friends, money, a house, a fat bank account, I am independent, hard-working and I am living it up, I don't need anything or anyone." If that is so, here's something to ponder, and think about with an honest and open mind, "Are you really satisfied deep down on the inside?" When you take the odds into consideration, "Are these things really giving you the desired happiness your heart craves?" My guess is that if you are truthful to yourself your answer would be '**No.**'

The fact is, no matter how much we may try to apply other things, which will seek to lessen the pain or hell we have faced, it's not going to give us the lasting satisfaction that we wish to embrace. Those things only serve as temporary assets but at the end of the day when we are alone, we tend to forget that the battlefield is in our minds. "What do we do then?" Most of us tend to push people aside. We become self centered, cold, bitter, isolated, with less desire to open up or give attention to corrective solutions. We often go into our comfort zones, thinking that no one understands. They don't know what we've been through or how hard it is. Sometimes we even get to the point where we don't want to be bothered. We often contemplate suicidal thoughts. Some turn to a drink, or anything that can easily quench the pain. Others keep trying to fool themselves into thinking that they'll be ok.

But the truth is, they are hurting more than anything else and would be wishing at that period for the pain and agony in their soul to go away. Amazingly, as women we would in some way still find the strength to get up and shake ourselves from all the baggage in order to go through life's journey no matter what comes our way. Oftentimes we don't care from where we get the strength, as long as there is a determination to move on we will gravitate towards it with all the remaining courage we have. Sad to say, there are some who may not make it this far because their wall has caved in and life becomes motionless.

In spite of all that was just said, try to keep your mind focused, still looking at yourself in the mirror. Now let me bring your mind to understand this truth, "Do you know that you are a *'Woman'*?" You may say well, it's obvious. May I invite you to take a closer look at comprehending what I really mean. Now when I say you are a '*Woman*', I am not just stating it from the physical sense or to the fact that you are good looking, classy, sassy, or just down to earth sexy and fine to the bone. Honey, if you delight or define yourself based on what I've just mentioned then go right ahead and smile because you are a Woman. However, I want you to take your eyes away from the physical side for a bit. I wish to open your mind to the understanding that you are a '*Woman*'. In fact, you were called **'Woman'** from the time your heavenly Father conceived you in your mother's womb and created you in His image and likeness. Therefore, let me humbly engage your attention towards recognizing that we were made in the image and likeness of God, knowing God is Spirit (*Gen 1:26, St. John 4:24*). Since that is so, it means that our whole being is not just composed of a physical structure but also a spiritual one.

Now, I want you to look in that mirror and face yourself with all you've got left in you. And declare to yourself by simply saying, "I've got to cherish my being as a '*Woman*'. Yes, say it aloud! And say it like you mean it, like if it's the last breath you have left. Trust me, that takes guts. Especially if you don't feel that way, nevertheless, go ahead and say it because you can't change what you already are. You are Woman!!!

When I say you are a '*Woman*', in spite of all the unfortunate circumstances that you've experienced, the heart aches, misery and pain, you are a '*Woman*' simply because God created you as one. Unquestionably, in every sense of the word '*Woman*' you are. The word woman connotes the idea of a human, a female, a whole spiritual design or being, framed holistically into creation, complete, and fitted uniquely. Although you may feel somewhat fragmented at this point, you are still whole. Even though you may be standing there in a being that is broken or shattered to pieces, just as a piece of glass, you are still whole.

Notice this one thing, when God created woman (*Genesis 2:18, 21-25*) He caused the man to fall asleep. God knew that man was unsatisfied, lonely, and that he needed companionship. Why? Because he was incomplete, living alone. Although he had everything he wanted he didn't have everything he needed as '**yet**'. The woman was the missing link! Are you following me here? At this point you really have to get it in your system that you are a *'Woman'* not based on what anybody says. It's not merely an outward physical appearance or component; you were constructively designed in the epitome of God's conception, perfected to complete His initial plan for creation. Neither is it dependent on what you think but rather who God says you are and created you to be.

After God caused the man to fall asleep, notice what He did next. He took a rib from the man and made *'Woman'*. Something was taken out of man for a woman to emerge. Why wasn't she created from dust just like the man? It's quite natural to think that God could have used anything else and perhaps used the same method as He used to create man (Adam). But knowing His ability to create, God decided to act spontaneously just so that we could marvel at His creation and the power He has to create. So God took a rib from the man **(not from his head or heel)** and when the woman was formed, after viewing her radiance, her charismatic beauty, her inconceivable appearance, knowing that He was well pleased, He presented this well made but fragile gift to man. As the man received and accepted this gift he called her '**Woman'.** Say this with me, *"There is power in being a Woman!"*

Can you imagine God himself had to take you from the most enveloped place of a man to form you? Well you may say it was just a rib, but was it just a rib? Ask yourself this mind-boggling question, What was in this '***Rib'*** that God decided upon and chose to use it? And then ask, "Why did Adam call me Woman?" You see, when God gave the woman to man and he called her Woman, God knew that she was complete, fit and ready to take up such a task as a woman. God knew that the rib He had removed from man had every potential to produce the excellence and flawless kind of woman He desired to form. She was crowned with a magnitude of beauty that man couldn't comprehend.

Remarkably, God presented woman to man, knowing that she was well established within her being as a woman, constructed and constituted for companionship and designed to be with man because she came out of him. She was the exact complimentary partner! For further emphasis, if I may add, one of the presenters at the January 2011 Vision Conference, coined the phrase '***Crescendo of creation***' when referring to this being called woman. I know some of the men may raise their eyebrows here, but just note, "who said it", a man. So men, please, no fighting. Not that I'm esteeming a woman above you, but it's for us to grasp the definition and volume of God's creation and to understand that God's hand of artistry made women in complete wholeness.

Every part of '***Woman***' was carved from the inside out, that is, from God's spiritual likeness and image into the form of the physical components and into the fragile structure of a being. No part was missing! Her design reflected every single means of identity that speaks volumes of her femininity which shows that the Creator has to be represented through this image based on His intentions and purpose for creation. If I were you, I would put on my dancing shoes and praise God for the awesome work He did on this being called woman- You. The Creator took time to create you just as fine as you are. Just imagine, without a woman given to Adam, he would have had to live alone and the whole human race would have stopped. It is no wonder that Adam referred to Eve as the *"Mother of all Living"* (Gen. 3:20). Women! Rejoice for what God has assigned to you, knowing His plans are perfect. Not that all of your sufferings are a part of His intentions, but surely He has created a way that allows us to rise above our circumstances and failures.

From within my own world of experiences, I've heard many remarks hurled at women. Especially if they fail to project themselves as the woman society deems them to be. There are many who from different cultures and backgrounds hold their heads in shame, simple because they are called women. There are some, who, for one reason or the other, are not seen as women and are not even recognized in that capacity. On the other hand, there are many others who struggle to come to terms with their own nature and identity as a woman.

In the Jewish culture, a woman was sneered at, ostracized and branded from society and sometimes put to death if she committed any unlawful act pertaining to sex *(John 8:1-11)*. Now, this thought always seems to amuse my intellect because I've often wondered, "What happened to the man involved?" Why should the Woman alone encounter the worst of shame? Weren't two parties involved when the act was committed? So why should the woman endure the pain of the shame any more than the man? Unfair isn't it! *(St. John 8:1-12).* The fact is, that was how society's laws in that culture were in that time. I guess we in the western culture can say thank God we are of a different era but some things aren't altogether right with our culture either.

In fact, there are women who still feel neglected, mistreated, and abused. Women who undergo tremendous pressure and have no voice for themselves. There are those who are held hostage or are perhaps in bondage due to parental constraints and rigidity, with the thought that they have to protect them, squeezing the very life from these women to become free, independent-minded, God-centered beings and robbing their poor daughters of their God-given freedom. In noting the word 'freedom', I am not talking about selfish or prideful freedom where a woman can do as she pleases. I am simply speaking of the freedom given to us by God wherein we can express our true image as women.

There are those who don't know what it's like to have friends, who don't know what real love is, who don't know what appreciation or a warm embrace feels like. There are those who haven't a clue as to who they are, because they have lost such an identity. There are those who have been scarred and labeled as nothing good and worthless to the point where giving up seems like the better option. More so, those who try to forget their shame but still suffer silently, waiting for the day when peace will reign. There are others who go through life as if they're cursed and cannot understand who they are. I mean women all over the globe can attest to so much that it seems as if hope is lost. Believe me! The list goes on and on.

In as much as being a woman is honorable, life in itself shows us that experiences can knock us down or out. Don't get me wrong here, I am not saying that it is altogether difficult in being a woman, it's just that many of us undergo various challenges that cause life to seem somewhat unfair and hard. However, if we take into consideration the creation order as it relates to God creating women, we would realize that God designed us in a particular way that is unlike man.

In doing so, He constructed an image that man can't even resist at certain points. Poor Adam himself was taken away by the beauty he beheld. I guess he was so amazed that his brain had to be in control to tell his eyes what to do. I am not too sure if as women we understand who we are and what we are made of and whether or not we comprehend our status, in the image of God as He designed us to be. Regardless of where we have been, no amount of hardship can define the character God intends for us to have in Him.

No marks or bruises, pain or frustration, failures or mistakes can define who we are in God. As long as He is the author of our lives, our record is clean before Him and even if He is not, He is awaiting the moment to clothe you in His grace. In spite of what the world may think, what people may say, no one knows who you are going to be and what you are going to become until God reveals His image in you through the reflection of His Son in you. You may come from the worst state of life, but that does not in any way define your future *(Jer. 29:11)*. Even when the prostitute or stripper is transformed in Christ, man cannot fathom what happened. Most assuredly, we should count the value of women as something God designed to impact society far more than we can imagine. We are not worthless infidels who have no purpose and no reason to exist. We exist because God is the author of life and not man. How odd that we forget that we were both created by God for His purpose.

The funny thing is, the eyes of those in the world will always be on the watch looking to see what you are going to be and what you will become. Furthermore, they cannot help since they have not a clue as to what you will become in Christ. My dear, hold on to the woman in you no matter what, because you are on the path of becoming. Just stay focused on you! Watch yourself in the mirror, and know that God is not through with you as yet. His work is just about to take root in your life. Amidst what you are seeing at the moment, note carefully all is temporary. This is not the complete you. Neither is it your final state, until you find completeness in Christ.

You may say to yourself "I don't want anybody to know about me, I'm comfortable where I am, nobody knows my troubles." But ask yourself this question, "How long do I intend to linger and feel pitiful towards myself?" "How long will I stay in this God-forsaken den and be miserable with myself?" Well then, I'll simply suggest that if you are up to the challenge to see the beauty in you and to come to a point of cherishing *'You'* as a woman, hold fast to your seatbelt and let's examine more. I implore you to read on, because this is only the beginning and I guarantee you that at the end of this book you will crave for change. The end is not yet, tarry and let's see the exact image God intends of you to possess.

Chapter 4

'Me- Through The Eyes Of The Mirror'

Your past is just a subtotal of who you are and if you refuse to deal with it, then you are giving that past a free rule over you, and you will dissolve the possibility of a future expression of your truth.

If we are not careful to address our past situations, we can find ourselves in an unusual slumbering position which could rip away our focus from the rest of reality. So often we can relate to attitudes we display, by being sluggish, weary, burnt out and confused as well as frustrated to the point that life ebbs away slowly, leaving us undone and used. Facing the mirror at this instance, may seem unbearable and even insurmountable. Although the load on the inside feels as if it's causing your body to wreak with unquenchable pain, standing in front of the mirror says, there's more to you than you can imagine. Yes, just the fact that you are there standing and looking at you, in all this agony, says your strength can push you to victory if you faint not. The key however, is not in self but in Christ. At this moment, let me take this opportunity to invite you into my personal closet so as to unveil certain intimate aspects of my past. These experiences will definitely help you to see that standing can do a lot, far more than what others may say, think or do.

Unquestionably, I was fortunate to be born into a family of initially seventeen offspring *(10 are presently alive)* born from the womb of a mother who had to toiled day and night to provide for us. I am the twelfth child and the only twin, born out of this lineage and on my father's side, I'm the first daughter. Actually, this fact only became significant later on in my life when my own world started to find meaning and balance. Sad thing is, while we were growing up as children our fathers never stuck around to give us the necessary support or parental guidance that we needed. As much as they contributed to our lives financially, to some extent, their absence spurred much internal and external injury. And it was so hard to see my mother wrestling with maintenance far less the load of parenting. From my estimation, I have always found it quite mind boggling for her to juggle with the responsibility of both parents' weight. Unfortunately, situations can cause such a twist where parents have to make hard decisions that would enable us to survive one way or the other.

Seems to me that this was my mother's portion daily, mainly when assistance from elsewhere hung on a dim horizon. My mother was practically a domestic worker on all ends. Watching her manned all of us was at times pretty unbearable to the eyes. In fact, life was just plain tough! On many occasions we had no choice but to resort to drinking water, if possible find fruits, like mangoes or bananas to quench the hunger on the inside of our stomachs. Things were pretty hard on us, so much so that we often descended on our relatives for a meal. We wore *hand-me-downs*, slept on each other and on the floor. We didn't know then what *"living in London"* was like, much less to even dream of going to London. Yet as a little girl, I would watch my mom struggle from day to day, simply fighting to see us become something of worth, someday.

I love the way she never gave up, believing that God would elevate us from all of those difficulties. She depended on her faith and would often discipline us in this area of life. Although my mother or siblings never became aware of this, I was mindful to take an interest in observing her faith, because to me, I was amazed at the way God would work things out when she prayed. Even when we would ask hard questions, the reply to such was always the same, *"Be patient, God will provide, don't worry"* or she would turn to one of her favorite songs and start to sing away, in her own world of hope. But to our surprise, those were the days when meals came, assistance from others, new clothes, and new shoes. Of course we were in glee when life granted us such ease from the stress it often brought to our lives. While my mother was not the best of mothers, who had the luxury of everything, such as, the finest job, the best of education, the perfect house or car. Her simple faith was enough. I must admit, times of desperation caused her to turn to the wrong end as well, which led my life into a world of misery.

At the age of six, life took a swirling turn into a direction that I never anticipated or dreamt. Life then, had its good and bad days. Therefore, growing up in the countryside as a young girl who possessed charm and beauty caused regrettable scars from men whose eyes waited in silence to devour the simple and fragile youth that existed within. In order for me to paint the picture clearly, regarding the above mentioned, let me explain a particular portion of my childhood to you. From the time I was able to recognize and understand the mind in me *(that is my own world on the inside)* I took pride in admiring the sacrificial nature of my mother's dedication and selflessness. She worked hard and I wished for the day when I would be able to put her hands to rest from all her labor. Obviously, my sisters and I were taught the normal routine of discipline, where chores and other responsibilities were concerned, so that we could grow up to be the apple of our mother's eye. I guess nothing would

[39]

be more pleasing to a dedicated mother. But to be honest, we often drifted from such expectations, especially me. I can remember the first time when I was shown the steps of washing my own clothes, along with the sister who was after me.

Actually, that particular sister and I grew up closer than my other sisters and were involved in doing all the chores together. During that period of being taught to do my own laundry, my mother became so irritable towards me because I didn't do it right the first time, and I got one good piece of whipping. In that instance, I remember her words to this day, *"How can you expect to be a wife if you can't look after a house, yet you prefer running around like a tomboy all over the place and not take interest in what is important?."* In fact, after hearing those words I tucked them away in my mind and would often wonder. "Why do I need to become a housewife? Was I not worth more than that? Or can't I be far more than what my mother thinks? How could a person just settle to be a housewife?"

I used to think that housewives were boring, people who failed to see themselves as nothing more, and I hated to think that I would become a housewife. I resented that with a passion! All this came as a result of seeing my own mother toiling for years and years, never having the experience to live beyond this routine. And I was determined not to even draw near that line in my life. I figured it was just total slavery with no early retirement in sight, much less freedom to live out your own desires. So I kept the thought in my head that I would never amount to a housewife, I would always strive to be more than what people think of me. Back then, being six was an advantage to me in some sense. Interestingly, I developed a fancy for the way boys operated instead of striving to learn the average ways of a normal girl. To me, it didn't seem strange, but in the eyes of those in society (*especially the women*), you would be labeled with a few choice words that negatively altered your freedom to *'Be'*. For some reason, if you were not domestically inclined, you will be seen as a lazy and an unfruitful young woman who may never be able to marry or have a pleasant home. Not that those thoughts diverted my mind, because in all truth, I enjoyed the fun of being a tomboy. Life in those moments seemed innocent and harmless, and I thought nothing of it, so I simply took it as a good, old fun ride. At least I would have preferred being in the streets playing cricket, football, riding a bicycle, chilling with the boys on the block rather than doing laundry, dishes, homework etc. To me, then, it wasn't a big deal until later on; I realized what mom's message truly meant.

Due to my mother's regular absence from the home due to the demands for provision, I became carefree. Unfortunately, I never grew up sheltered or protected to the extent where I felt safe and loved as a cuddled teddy bear. Life was open and my older brothers and sisters were placed in the responsible position to monitor those of us who were younger but that didn't stop us from having our own way at times. I guess the old saying, **"When the cats are out, the mice comes out to play"** fits this scenario quite well. Although my mother's efforts were creditable, the absence of my father and being a twin affected me silently. Honestly, I never talked about this or shared how much it played on my mind.

There were instances when I felt as if I had to live for my deceased twin. That in itself, brought me to the point where the nature of adopting a tomboy's lifestyle, along with acting carefree, resulted in serious injuries to my youthful life. I blindly pursued this gravitation towards the tomboy nature so as to avoid all that had to do with living as a young lady, but never realizing the dangers lurking at my door. Shadowing that part of me was natural, until it grew into a mood of resistance from wanting to be a girl. No one knew those thoughts circulated in my mind, and to me, adopting this nature was far better than being a normal young lady. At times, I fought to balance myself, and every time I observed my mother, it drew me further and further from ever wanting to be anything that she projected as a woman.

I only saw a woman in slavery and I thought that if this was what being a woman was, I wanted no part of it. I preferred the thought of being a tomboy and I began to swallow this idea as I lived secretly in my own mind and world. Living and adapting to such a fantasy was no real challenge. It came quite easily and naturally. I mean, I did the obvious, the works of a *"tomboy"*- playing cricket, football (soccer) in the road, riding bicycles, climbing trees, pitching marbles, spinning tops, I mean, every game a boy knew, I had to get in on the fun. I did this so often that forfeiting my house chores became a regular habit with the punishment at the end, and that I didn't mind at all.

In my mind, I wished I was a boy and being one was at that point far better to me than being a girl, because boys in my opinion were more adventurous, out-going, competitive, smarter and good company. Girls, in my mind, were too petty, always crying for the silliest things, and too emotional. And I hated to feel or to even see myself as one. In essence, I just wanted to be what I felt without anyone telling me that I could not be. So, embracing male company was a way to project the *'tomboy'* attitude, to avoid being around girls too often and of course thinking and acting like them became quite natural. So much so, that I didn't recognize the trap ahead of me, that the devil was planting, all along.

Eventually, I started to become intrigued with my sexuality, always looking at stuff I shouldn't. Strangely enough, my brother's curiosity about girls stirred my interest. They would often bring videos and magazines that were prohibited, containing pornography, and at that time I hadn't the slightest clue about what I was getting involved in. Certainly, I dared myself to view all and to even read the books and watch the movies as they came. Finding them was easy, because they were stocked in areas that mom was unable to detect. I would find them under the bed, amongst the clothes, hidden in drawers and amidst underwear. And I looked for these while the *'Cat'* was out, so to speak. No one knew of my secret interest, but as time advanced, it started to take a swirl in my mind, leaving me with realities of regrettable taste.

At the age of six, I encountered my first cycle of sexually related activities through molestation. That experience brought about a whole spiraling of complex thoughts and emotions that just sent me into a cocoon. I can recall well, the beatings I received for not knowing how to explain what had happened to my mother, more so for being afraid. I was like a jigsaw puzzle, trying to understand what had taken place, as well as, finding the words to relate my emotions to my mother. So instead, I coiled into myself and just accepted my punishment. What bothered me most at that point was the lack of outright care, affection and understanding that came from my mother. Not that I didn't want to tell her what had happened but by not seeing that motherly affection to withdraw the information from me that she needed and worse yet beating me so harshly; I grew worse, into myself. I am not blaming her necessarily for the actions she took. Any mother would in some way resort to a quick whipping without thinking straight, since they would be agitated by a non-responsive child who was gripped by fear and could not explain herself, or more so the ignorance of dealing with such a child. Yet what I hoped for was to see her clothed me in her arms with love until I was able to find the words to tell her the whole story, but that was just a distant thought. My mother only did what she knew and it caused me to build a level of resistance and distance.

As time went by, I became quite promiscuous, getting molested and involving myself with one male after the other. Sadly, some of the returns were monetary in some cases. Honestly, I had no idea as to what came over me with such force that even when I wanted to quit, I was trapped. What haunted me the most, was the thought that some of these males were my relatives as well as my mother's cohabited friends. I cannot begin to tell you how these incidents robbed me of my femininity and childhood. All through those periods of my life, I was drowned into the tomboy lifestyle, clothing the little bit of who I was, not wanting to be touched or hurt. I began to shelter myself, yearning for rescue while no one knew the turmoil I suffered inwardly. I never went to my mother or siblings, no one. I simply kept those affairs to myself, except when my mother found out and then the whip became my fate. One primary incident, I can recall, shook my mindset with a desire to be different and wanting out from all of this mess. Because to me, all I could feel was a little girl trapped in a web, not knowing how to find a window of escape.

My mother cohabited with a man of whom we had little information about or had any clue to when she started seeing them. Actually, in my mind, this was her custom, since she hardly made mention of her affairs until they showed up at our door. Nonetheless, that was my mother's way of doing things. Eventually, she moved in with this particular guy and took along my sister and I. At that point, we were preparing for primary level final exams *(Common Entrance)*, so the books had us going. Up to this day, I have no idea how I functioned in school.

One evening, mom requested that we come to the house where the man lived; since she was spending time there while working at the hospital as a female attendant *(a janitor who cleans and assists in the kitchen area of the hospital)*. My sister went ahead of me, but I had this stirring gut feeling not to even enter the house that evening. Finally when I got there, I crept to the bedroom window where I realized my mother was since the window was opened. And I peeped to see if she was nearly ready for work. There she was ironing and quarreling about me not adhering to her instructions and was most upset because my sister was earlier than me. I listened and concocted a story which I knew was a total lie, just to escape her whipping. Believe me, it worked.

After this, she got dressed and left for her night duty at the hospital, leaving the two of us at home with her friend. At first, I wanted to return home, but I knew my sister would not give in, lest she suffered beatings as well. But at that point in time, I really didn't care about the whipping. All I knew in my guts is that uneasy feeling of something was about to happen. I couldn't detect what it was at the exact moment, but I knew. You know what, I was right. At about midnight, I was nowhere near sleep due to the discomfort in my spirit. My sister was fast asleep, all lost to what was happening within me, so I just watched outside the window. Believe it or not my mother's friend came into the room. He took my hand and carried me off to his bedroom without my sister realizing anything. I wanted to scream and yell, but it was useless. The truth is, I did not want my sister to be touched or get hurt, so I went along with his biddings. Mind you, I didn't go ahead with any thought as to what all this would bring about in my life at a later period. For some reason, I was just absent minded about the implications of all these sexual activities. Truth be told, I was clueless and without wisdom. As a matter of fact, at that point, I was not able to bear the burden of seeing my sister hurt as I was about to. I took the fall instead.

Throughout that night, I was like a wife to a husband. Afterwards, he assured me that no one would know and it would be kept a secret. The following morning, my sister sensed that something was wrong when she caught me coming out from his bedroom. I froze in my tracks, eyes knitted! And the question came, full blown, *"What were you doing in that bedroom and why were you not in your own bed?"* "I am going to tell mommy as soon as she comes home." I was twelve years old and in the valley of a nightmare. As appalling as this was, he gave us money to keep his filthy secret, but my sister insisted and went and spilled the beans. I went through a series of trauma that day; to the Courts to file a complaint, the doctor's office, received beatings and faced the mockery of it all from my fellow siblings and neighbors. I felt so crushed, bewildered, bewitched and so empty as if love had suddenly escaped all hope of finding me again. While I understood that better was expected of me, knowing that my mother was trying to afford us a sense of livelihood, the absence of love hit every nerve in me like a rocket. From then, I started living as a loner and masquerading in the tomboy nature in order to protect whatever was remaining in me as a young girl. My world was no pretty sight to behold.

I adapted a low self esteem, no real value, no sense of worth for who I was. In essence, I gave up on me and I wanted out of life. My world of innocence and femininity were destroyed and I didn't know how to reverse the clock, so I sought suicide at age thirteen. No one knew of my intentions because I was home alone. In all of my emotional, psychological, physical and sexual traumas, not once did my mother counselled me as a child. Not that I'm blaming her for my errors, but more so to help you see how often parents can be ignorant and may need help as well. At one time, I was beaten so badly by her until she stated her hatred for me as her daughter. I was a wrecked ship. My father was not in my life and I had no real parental guidance to govern my life directly. We were sent to church, yes! But little did I understand what part church played in my life and the pivotal role it was or should be.

All of the absentees in my life caused me to drift into a world of my own, to the point that when I felt unloved, I searched for it myself but ended up hurting. In my family, I only did what house chores were given to me and kept to myself for the most part. I locked away all my fears, troubling moments and even when things happened, I just stored them away and resorted to something that distracted me so as not to focus on the pain. Silently, I was dying but somehow managed to keep going at life, determined to make a difference. Ask me why? I had no immediate clue. Yet, deep within my mind, I just wanted to change into something that would erase the haunted house I lived in.

As absurd as this is, one of my very own siblings sought to beguile me into having sex with him for $10 (E.C). The end result of that trauma was finding a knife to protect myself because in all honesty, I would have killed him in cold-blood had he returned with such ridiculous intent. Here, again, my mother was absent from home and was not told of this until sometime later. However, what brought about the worst of scars in my life was when my mother again lived with another of her cohabited friends. But this time though, his brother tried trapping me in his own house, claiming I should *"Give up my goods and he has a right to rape me."* The rage that filled my mind, I almost stabbed him. Oddly enough, it was his sister who had the silent prying eyes.

She was very close to my mother due to her mother's illness. My mother assisted and ended up living there, and of course she took my sister and me. Sixteen, and wandering in life, she became that person who I grew to talk to about almost anything, a confidant, a mother figure, a caregiver; one who treated me well. And honestly, I welcome this difference because I wanted to feel and experience a sense of belonging, a place where I didn't have to feel unwanted or mistreated. Granted, she showed care in relation to my well being, but little did I know that her reasons bore sexual enticement. My sister and I were often supported financially by her during our schooling especially when my mother was unable to meet such needed demands.

In fact, I was given preferential treatment as they say, but had I known of her secret spell, I guess my life would not have endured the relentless agony following the aftermath. Secretly, I was brought into her private closet with no awareness of her intentions. I was too blind to see, since my deepest quest at that moment was finding love and happiness. So she eventually introduced me into her chambers of sexual pleasure. Again, my sister became the open door for the news to reach my mother's ear, but this time, the beatings left me badly wounded, had not the same man she was with taken her off me.

If I could give you an honest reason as to how I got this far, I would be telling you the biggest lie. To me, I was just accepting the love that was shown to me and in return I simply loved back the way love appeared to me then. Perhaps I was too messed up to even define what love really meant and when I received it I thought it was some sort of prized possession, so I reached for it with all my heart. Being introduced to such a lifestyle at the age of sixteen, I figured it was real and that was what I deserved, so I embraced the encounter without thinking that this was a spirit of lesbianism I invited to humbly abide in me. I had absolutely no clue and for those who may think I should have known better, please understand that when love appears in your eyes from a conditional state or expression, especially when you've searched to know it, but have a limited definition, you'll misrepresent the very idea of it.

The entire surfacing of this grew to the community awareness which didn't make life easier at all. I was heckled, ridiculed and often seen as some sort of prize tag for men's easy picking. I was not at peace within my community and though I kept to myself little associations and few friends, it didn't help with the frustration and isolation I felt deeply. I tried hard to fit in wherever I went and in anything I was a part of, but it was the more difficult life became and I adapted all the more into the tomboy fantasy. For me, in these spaces, at least that was where I felt an unwavering sense of safety. Although some folks treated me partially fair, my own family saw me in the eyes of shame, and that pain ached my soul beyond. I kept wondering what was wrong with me, and what would it take for me to be different, because my sister was the one who was applauded for everything, while I had to settle for the crumbs on the table. Believe me, the thought to turn around from all this filth was not only a deep desire, but also a matter of trying to please my mother, since she saw me as the one who brought her shame and disgrace. If I were to recall all of my life experiences, I would not be able to get to the bottom of the message I wish to convey to the woman in you. Yes! I agree, my story holds quite an unbearable and agonizing scenery, but for some reason I endured it all.

Even though I accepted Christ at the age of thirteen, I found that the folks at church were no different to those outside. Interestingly, when I truly needed rescue and thought this was my safe haven, they only saw me as the girl who was the tomboy who had no good report. The funny thing is, my home church was made up of numerous family members. While some tried to talk me out of these traumatic occurrences, they did so from an average thought and not an educational template. Some even rebuked me sternly with the hope that I would change, yet lacked the level of discernment to see my world from my perspective and it wasn't any easier to apply their suggestions or well intended opinions. I just didn't know how, much less where to begin or even how to change on my own. Therefore, in my own mind, I never really saw the need to make the extra effort to change as they recommended. I was the one who resigned myself to observing things from a distance and only availed myself when asked. Otherwise, I was just a member in the congregation searching for love, with a broken and defiled life. Besides the youth department, and the activities of which I was rarely a part because in their eyes, I wasn't seen as the clean or righteously attired young lady, I went to church just for church keeping sake. Nevertheless, I desired a great deal to be different. Inwardly, I was tired of seeing my world shattered, broken, lonely, unloved, miserable, unhealthy and unclean. If I was not molested, I was taken advantage of, seduced with money and left to figure out who I am or what was at the core haunting my life with such venom.

Silently, I suffered throughout these experiences, and for years I kept them from my mother's knowledge. Not for the sake of not wanting her to know or share in my pains, but it would have never been void of the whip or some verbal expressions and insensitivity to my soul. At that point, I had enough!! Enough of the insults, the demeaning expressions, the whip, the lecturers that left me sore to the core, the uneducated counsel… Name It!! I grew tired and figured enduring was safer. I battled how I could, and just survived whatever the day issued without thinking. Yet, strangely, each day I would find the courage to pray in secret places; *the toilet, the bathroom, in the fruit trees, in the grass areas where no one could see me and even in the church when my cousin and I went to do the cleaning.* These spaces provided some of the most exhaling levels of refuge, where I could breathe separate and apart from everything and everyone. I was desperate and desired freedom from all these demons that haunted my life. If I am to sum up my mindset then, I would say that I was in a world of blinded forces that ripped my life right in front of my eyes. It seemed as if there was a veil covering my whole life from living in any sense of the word, happiness or peace *(My Eden)*. At times I felt as if I was living someone's curse or punishment of sexual disorientation or dysfunctional system, as if I had to bear the consequences of their errors while there was nothing I could do about it or about making my life any better.

However, I will say this to all who are reading this book right now, although you may identify with my past in one way or the other, note this one thing well, change is possible and no matter what may be keeping you from finding internal peace, God's arms are wide open to cleanse every part of you and to transform you into the woman He created you to be. I thought my life was earmarked for destruction through sexual promiscuity and while I did not have the defense mechanism to ward off these forces that sought to destroy my life, I never knew that those simple prayers I prayed were the catalyst to provide the breakthroughs that turned my life into the greatest testimony today .

I must admit that coming out wasn't the easiest journey. Oftentimes as a young believer, who was looking for a way of escape, I failed to upkeep my faith in Christ due to a lack of genuine guidance, understanding or substantive support. I had no personal mentors or private counselors *(except for a few persons who tried to talk with me and who in their best efforts aided in whatever way they could, of which I am grateful today)* who sought my interest to the extent of helping to shape my life into the woman God intended. All I knew was that I wanted a way out from my personal dungeon and to experience the beauty and dignity of being a woman.

It was not until the age of eighteen that I started to press into knowing God for myself in addition to what I learned at church, home and school, as well as other places. In as much as I was introduced to Him through my pastor's teachings and others who encouraged me in the Word, for what it's worth, I wanted to know God for myself. I figured that personal encounter, that one on one experience was the ideal forum for me to really realize that He was reachable and had my best interest at heart. I wanted that personal reality without anyone having any part in it. I wanted to know God for God, not what was preached about Him, taught about Him, or even scripted about Him. My mind was at a place where I somehow knew and believed, if I had one moment, one encounter with Him, He would mend the wounds within me. Without any sense of doubt, fear, or wavering I pursued God with my all.

On the eve of writing my final exams *(Secondary Level)*, I was in one of my secret closets, *the toilet*, with my bible, and I began my devotional segment for the day. In spite of my internal rifts, I wanted my schooling to produce something which my mother would be proud of, as well as, to show that it was a stepping stone to be different, more so, to prove I had what it took to become somebody *(Psalm 27:10)*. I became adamant about this sudden quest because I saw it as my only hope.

During my devotional period, I began calling on God to heal my wounds, to heal my heart from the pain, to make me into the woman He created me to be, I cried and cried. I admitted all of my errors, failures and shame. I recalled being so drenched in my tears, filled with immense grief and pain, Elizabeth's prayer suddenly came to mind. *"Thus the Lord has dealt with me, in the days when He looked on me, to take away my reproach among people." (Lk 1: 25).* This prayer consumed me with a volume of intensity I cannot describe, and mind you it was not even a scripture I knew.

[53]

I kid you Not!! All I knew was, as I prayed with fervency and an honest regard, my entire being was enveloped by the Holy Spirit. Right then and there, I remember saying *"God if you take my reproach from among men, I don't care if I do not get married, I will serve you for the rest of my life."* I even ventured into making a deal with God on the basis of at least passing five of my subjects *(CXC)*. It was a cry from the depth of my heart and a dying need for transformation. At that moment, during all the tears, I wasn't even aware of the still small voice that spoke so vividly. Oh yes!! He did.

That day marked an encounter which I have shared over and over wherever I ministered. It was so clear and so real that I almost jumped off the toilet seat because of bewilderment. I couldn't believe God responded. I heard this audible response, ***"Please turn to Isaiah 55 and this will be my covenant with you, so I was with David and made Him a witness and leader of nations, so I will do with you, if you believe."*** I humbly sought the chapter and began reading its invitation to those who are thirsty to come and drink of the salvation God provided. I needed no other evidence to show me that God heard the faintest cry of those who are broken and wounded, left to find life's meaning on their own. He became real that day and began working on the inside of my heart, soul, mind, spirit and body. He lifted me from shame to abundant life and now I am able to share with you the reality of His love so that you can be redeemed into the woman He created you to be. Believe it or not, my prayers were answered and I got my subjects. Even though no one believed in me, God did, and He saw beyond the scars, brokenness and shame, the future He predestined for me. It was hard being a wrecked and torn apart ship for years. Therefore, I can well imagine how difficult it is for you even as you read these pages.

Regardless of your tumultuous internal agony, God knows who you are even before you were born *(Jer.1:5)*. In fact, He knows that your destiny awaits you if you simply call on His name. Your past is just a subtotal of who you are and if you refuse to deal with it, then you are giving that past a free rule over you forever, and you will dissolve the possibility of a future expression of your truth. It will rob you of what was intended for you to partake of, that which has life and liberty for your every need. Conscientiously, you're aware of your past as it is, but doing nothing about it will frustrate your internal and external worlds. Anyone who may come in contact with you will suffer the consequences of your failure to deal with your past. Do you know why? It's a simple reason, it will produce attitudes, so much so, that it will create havoc even in the silent corridors of your soul.

You can choose to be silent about it - Like I did. And somehow expect a miracle of escape from it all as the years roll by. But the sad thing is, it will always find room to stir misery. As the saying goes, *"Misery loves company"*. So the question is, "What are you going to do about your past?" Live in it or get out of it! The truth is, every single person on the planet has a past of some kind. Although the conditions may vary, we cannot erase the fact that succumbing to the same emotions, such as pain, hurt, brokenness or any related suffering with what I have faced cannot happen to you. Some may even be more excruciating and may find it unbearable, so suicide becomes the saddened ultimatum. Furthermore, when we fail to come to terms with our past issues, we often disregard the truth, especially when it touches our core and sores. Rather than facing the light in order to see where we went wrong and finding solutions to aid our troubles, we resist and make room for disaster.

My friends, or should I say ladies, we were given the opportunity to live one life and I believe that all of us would hope to live it at our best. But in order to do so holistically and to find meaning and purpose, we cannot refuse the need for God's divine intervention. It is only through Him that our past experiences can be redeemed and given back a hope brighter than the darkness that once consumed you. So let us embark on this pursuit to discover what God intended when he created us as women. Let's delve into the scriptures to unleash the magnitude of beauty within the confines of this structure called woman. "Are you ready to unveil your closet in order to find such meanings?" Why not journey with me to the end of this book.

Chapter 5

'Emptying Your Closet'

I would like to think that had Eve seen a glimpse of the devil's mental image concerning her future, she would have dropped the fruit without further discussion.

As uncomfortable as this may be, many of us tend to shy away from dealing with our failures simply because we prefer the short term and expensive *'easy fix'* instead of coming to grips with the reality of our issues. It is always easy (or so we *seem to think)* to keep our hurts inside rather than finding resolve through- God, a pastor, a counselor or a trust-worthy friend to guide us into proper decision making processes. In availing yourself to obtain help from such persons, you will be giving yourself a better opportunity to live more comfortably, instead of suffering alone. Please do not sit there and whine about, "Who will understand me? Who will listen or who will understand my pain?" Sinking into such a *'pity party'* syndrome, while allowing your life to be festered with grievous sores and giving room for live maggots to dwell happily. Honey! This is obviously not going to solve anything until you get up and decide to do something about it. Trust me! You can cry all you want but self pity will not help you to see the light at the end; it is only when you get up *(come to your senses in your mind)* that you will be able to do something about the mess you're in and give change its rightful place.

Dealing with YOU *(Internally)* will force that natural and spiritual ability to look beyond your frail structure since it is the internal rift that has been dividing your very life and leaving you in pieces, instead of becoming whole, well seasoned, matured and God defined individuals. So many of us wander around with all kinds of trauma from our past or even present circumstances. We are too blind to realize that they will soon destroy us and leave us as hollow and lifeless humans. If we are to progress intentionally and see ourselves in God's image, there are certain steps that we will have to undertake in order to bring back that blissful, dazzling, impeccable and enthralling feminine character deeply embedded within.

I can recall on many occasions when I would have been in the same position and felt as if no one understood my world. Oftentimes, I wished for someone to hear my voice, my wailing, my pain and even my internal screams just so that I could find harmony with myself and others. But no matter the amount of cries that were echoed, no one heard, and it left me sinking since I had no desire to help myself. All I did was keep the pain alive day after day and waited for the day when light would shine.

How foolish was I to think like that, while my internal world was suffering and dying slowly. Women, please wake up and smell the coffee! You can holler all you want but until you decide to reach out for help it is just not going to always come easily or by some means of osmosis. Stop shutting yourself in some God forsaken closet and cause a stench that will slowly kill your own soul, body and spirit. That is more bait for the enemy to lead you into a natural course of deception and eventually, death. It is no wonder then that none can come into your world when it is so toxic and unhealthy. As hard as it may sound, you are the one who is killing you, no one else but *YOU*.

I've often wondered, why is it that when we are in such positions we simply crumble and succumb to our own faulty illusions. Think about it! Every emotion that we experience in this period is as a result of us choosing to remain where we are. Your choice simply creates or breaks. Let's go back to Eden for a bit. When God formed woman from man He used a part of man's appendage, a rib, to be precise. Grasp this well ladies, the rib reflected a joining that was cemented firstly, in the *"Spirit Of Man- The God Centered Being Of Man- Man As ONE"*, signifying that essential wholeness that man had before the woman was formed. Man in this regard was not merely an idea of God's imagination, and the rib in itself was not a physical entity. It was a metaphorical concept which takes us into the womb of creation. Adam- Male man, was put to sleep by God himself. This sleep was not a physical expression, but a by-product or a pro-type of God's conscious existence, in Himself, a place where Adam had no clue of how creation took its course- how Eve was formed.

The wholeness encapsulated here was all that God desired for us to recapture, since we lost our hold in the Garden of Eden. This *'Oneness'* in the form of a woman is what each and every woman ought to desire. That's the place we've lost and have every right to repossess but we will lose it if we choose to give it away to the wolves of our day. Don't be fooled! The devil cannot take anything from you unless there's an opening you've left unprotected. He cannot just barge in our doors and lay claim to our territories without us first failing to realize our blessings. If we leave our lives open, then the devil has every right to walk in himself and knock us out or down, flat on our faces, leaving us to clean up the mess. If we're not careful he'll return as often as he likes, until we choose to let God take full control of our lives.

Eve wasn't mindful of what she would have lost, since she was so caught up in the reasoning game with the devil. She completely, or should I say blatantly, disregarded God's directive. It was not until the devil made a stirring mess that she came to her senses but it was too late. The sin had already been committed. The deal was signed and well signed, because it left us at a place searching, trying to redefine who we are and whose we are. I would hate to think that Eve wasn't in any way sorry for her actions. Although she tried to play the blame game, God would not have it. I pause here to say this to the young women who may be contemplating all sorts of ideas as to how to win a man or control your destiny, or more so, to live life as you deem best for yourself. Stop right there in-your tracks! If you are honest enough and look closely in the mirror for yourself; you will realize that you are no worse than Eve. Instead of getting all self righteous, thinking that you have it made, consider God's judgment over your head. You may say to yourself, *"I didn't do what Eve did or I was not the one who lost it, she did"* but before you go on babbling your mouth off, just pause and think of this truth, from where did you originate and what does Eve mean? Get the picture? Just in case you act with some sort of amnesia, remember, God cursed all three persons involved; meaning judgment was passed on all.

You may think that you can run off and go about things in your own way, be sure to know that, sin has no regard for anyone and neither does the devil. And mind you, certainly, God would not let sin escape rightful correction. Note this carefully, regardless of how you may try to out think or out smart the devil, he will simply use you at all costs to get the job done, signed, sealed and delivered. Shake off the dust! It is not worthwhile to keep, and besides, why would you wish to carry around such baggage all day. Don't you know that they will eventually harness diseases and ultimately lead to your death, on every level.

I am confident that no woman on earth would wish to stay in a hole, wrapped around with all sorts of thistles not knowing how to untwine herself. Surely death will not pass her by unnoticed. Therefore, we have to make up our minds that regardless of the situations in our lives, God is our ultimatum for change. There are no two ways about it.

Tell me now, how would you go about emptying your closet? First of all, "What do you have hidden inside, that you wish no one else to see or know, but you?" Is it lies, thief, suicide, deception, incest, rape, fornication, adultery, homosexuality, envy, malice, jealousy, pride, anger, hate, or murder? "What is it?" It's up to you as I said before, to face the mirror. My dear, it's quite ok if all you see is guilt or shame. Of course we can be remorseful as long as it is genuine. The fact is, you are opening the closet and when you do, that is signifying your intentionality for change, deep down inside. Go right ahead, and take that bold step of faith and open it! If it pains like hell, scream if you have to, God is right there waiting for that moment to heal your wounded heart.

Do not let fear endanger your freedom here, because if you do, then it will promote its living organisms to haunt you far more than you can imagine. This is one of the most crippling tools of the devil's trade, which he masks so skillfully that you would not entertain the least thought of wanting to let go and let God. Do you know why? He will remind you every second of something that you did and paint it so perfectly and force you to see yourself just as that and nothing better. Lady!! That's the shadowing of death- *that imagery or illusion carved by fear,* presented with such a sink at its tail, you won't even recognize without discernment. This shadowing right here, pools your emotions in loops, and emphasizes a kind of triggering that will numb your soul. He will play on your emotions with every seductive language to erase your mental faculties from tapping into God's image and likeness. Furthermore, he will present what attracts you; something that will lure you into his web of deception. As difficult as it may be, you cannot afford to allow the devil to win the war on the inside of you, lest you believe his lies and send your soul to hell, easily. Greater is He that is in you than He that is in the world *(1 John 4:4).* I am imploring you to let go and let God. He is your ticket to a new beginning.

In fact, what many of us fail to understand here is that the internal struggles we are trying to combat are derived from external forces that are eating away our spirit from functioning in the divine order as initiated by God. Therefore, the devil will distract our attention from realizing the existing power that can ultimately liquidate his intentions toward us. He will never feed us with good stuff without some sort of compromise or counterfeit in the end. Surely he dresses up everything that he presents to us, in order to captivate our minds from seeing the true picture. Eve speaks very clearly here! He comes to do three specific things, steal, kill and destroy *(St. John 10:10).* So my sister, if you stay within your comfort zone and settle for the horrendous tricks of the devil, then you are simply giving eternity away without any consideration for the real meaning of life beyond living physically. Be mindful that the enemy is very subtle, crafty and cunning, and there is no reasoning that you can bring to match his already well carved intellect. In this area you are powerless without God's intelligence, wisdom and intervention.

I would like to think that had Eve seen a glimpse of the devil's mental image concerning her future, she would have dropped the fruit without further discussion. But that goes to show that not even our sense of reasoning, power or logic can be an element of challenge for the devil, on our own. This was where Eve faltered terribly, not that she wasn't intelligent or knowledgeable, nonetheless wise but what made her succumb was the thought of becoming more than what God said. Notice the twist in the statement to what the devil repeated in comparison to what God actually said to Eve. *"Then the serpent said to the woman, "You will not surely die. For God knows that in the day you eat of it your eyes will be opened, and you will be like God, knowing good and evil"* (*Genesis 3: 4-5*). Now compare this to Genesis 2: 16-17, *"And the Lord God commanded the man, saying, "Of every tree of the garden you may freely eat; but of the tree of the knowledge of good and evil you shall not eat, for in the day that you eat of it you shall surely die."*

Had Eve recognized the error in the devil's statement, she would have corrected him instead, but I guess she was too busy trying to become like God from the enemy's script. God never told Eve about her eyes opening if she ate the fruit. Not that He wasn't aware of the implications of her eating, but the important lesson for Eve to grasp was obedience rather than striving for power to become like God. Truth is! She was already made in *"His image and likeness"*- The essence of God himself. Hence the reason why sudden destruction fell on the earth and sin reigned in its full measure. Now for those of you who go around blaming Eve for where we are today, in terms of sin, remember, God provided the antidote, salvation. Ladies, please open your eyes, think on this, you are without excuse from accepting the priceless gift of salvation.

What made me unravel all of the above again, hmmm, I believe in all honesty, it's for the sake of aiding you with the understanding and importance of the position you're taking, ignorantly. Most convincingly, I would hate to know that the devil wins the battle over your life, based on the problems bombarding you. Therefore, emptying your closet or in other words your world of struggles, pains, burdens, worries or heartaches, however you choose to view them, becomes vital to finding liberty. Remember, in spite of the critical state you're in, God's mercies are new every morning *(Lam. 3:22-23)*. He will pour Himself in the most amazing ways on you, even when you're alone and cold, not knowing where the rest of the world has gone. Once you yield yourself to Him, confessing, taking, accepting and appropriating your issues; I mean really letting Him in on all the secrets and covered areas that were not revealed to others; the light will dispel the darkness you thought was so insurmountable. It is only through His blood you can truly be free, not in anything else and the sooner you come to realize this truth, the better you will understand His love for you.

In my years of fighting with my closet and trying to balance life otherwise; I realize much more weight was added when I simply kept the closet closed. My mind was overworked, my muscles were sore, my emotions were constantly seeking comfort and my surroundings were hateful because to me I did not fit in and my family was always on my back. No matter where I looked, life had something to add to the already confused world in which I was living. I believe it's no easier for you. Whatever source of comfort you may settle for at this point, note that it will only last for a period, and eventually you will look for another because you are not at peace with '*You*'.

The funny thing is, if those around you are not careful you will lash out at them and cause more harm than good, be it your husband, children, friends or co-workers. This unhealthy attitude, in the end, will steal your livelihood and destroy any remaining fragments that may be keeping you afloat. Sin has its own agenda and when it is not dealt with immediately life will be a constant zone of misery. Beloved, you will have to face YOU!!! That inner man, that person in the inward parts, who will suffer in a place where your spirit is unable to be expressed at maximum capacity. Listen! Ladies, no one will suffer in this world like you. This internal world in any state of silence will defuse your ability to see creation in any higher sense of reign or dominion. In other words, you will lessen your ability to *Become, Be and have your Being* in the truth of who God says you are, the originality of YOU.

In all honesty, it will not be the best sight, version or vision for you to behold, especially when you step in front of the mirror and view your closet, your world within. Your issues will show you nothing more than the reality it reveals. Ladies! The mirror cannot lie and will not lie for you. In this instance, I humbly empathize but the truth is you will have to empty your closet if change is what you are determined to possess through Jesus Christ. Yes, I know standing alone aches and the numbness in itself feels terribly crippling. However, taking that step to release all that's inside your closet will certainly bring about a light that will surely recompense all the hell you have been through. Start emptying yourself and let God open your eyes to the beauty He longs to harness in your character, anew. Let Him bring you into the deserving redefinition of your image and likeness, that eternal composite and design of the organic and original YOU. Go ahead lady! Let go and Let God!

Chapter 6

'Seeing You As God Sees You'

Ladies, we are all God's precious blueprint and amidst our struggles or pains, God's eyes are never short sighted about who we are in Him. We are the ones who easily lose that sight especially when we caused ourselves to believe that we could make it on our own.

Now, you've passed through the hardest route and dealt with those unbearable issues, as they were, by uprooting them and letting God's grace bring newness into your hearts. Let us now examine how the woman in you can take a dazzling effect with such an expression that others will wonder what just happened. I will admit though, that cleaning up will exercise some muscles which cannot just be on a physical level but more so - *A spiritual one.* Before you came to this point you were battling on a physical scale but as of now, you need to tap into your spiritual reservoir because this is where your alliance and military garments are found. So honey, guard every part of you with God's armor, since the devil will find any means to redirect your tracks in the old path you once trod. (*Eph. 6:10-11)*

Therefore, it's imperative for us to focus closely on the initial stages of the introduction of woman at creation. For us to intimately comprehend our being and its intrinsic value to humanity, we cannot disregard the divine order of our creation, lest we fail to see the reality of sin's enticement and appeal to our nature. Now, the truth is, overcoming will cause us to flex our muscles intensely because of the need to see ourselves on a totally different scale, that which depicts the newness thereof.

In particular, our spirituality will be the mending bridge regarding our newness or rather our identity being made anew. There are instances when seeing yourself as you once were, will present images or mental pictures that will be repulsive and impulsive. You may feel as if change is nowhere near, but I want to assure you that such hideous thoughts come as a result of the enemy trying to dissuade your mind from appreciating and valuing your identity.

Coming to terms with your dignity as a woman, can be a trying and painful process, since your situations may have consequences that may somehow seem intolerable. Yet, there are others who may find it not so difficult to make the necessary transition spiritually, but the important lesson for us here is to embrace ourselves right where we are. Nope! Don't try to put anything in there too quickly. This embracing holds more to you. So, rather than swallowing the past and relapsing into a state of deception, that which is able to repeat history, it's crucial for you instead to come to an understanding as to what God made you to be.

Herein lies many assets which can lead your life unto a journey, to experience the totality of your womanhood, in accordance with God's grace, on a daily basis. Although our past affects us tremendously and can be reversed in various ways, we are the ones who have to be mindful not to entertain any possible traits that may present themselves. No amount of reminiscing and cuddling of the images that may show up in our minds can give us the desired composure that we need to live in the divine order of our womanhood. We will have to work on every area, no matter how small or great they may be in our eyes. This is where we will see our redefinition and its worth as to what we can become in Christ.

However, before I venture off into the Genesis of woman coming into earth, let me help you understand why it is so essential for us to capture this newness, effectively. Now, we cannot ignore the fact that salvation is a continual process, and its defining art-work demands our entire commitment. Just as God covenanted with the Israelites in the beginning, so too you were grafted into this said covenant through Jesus Christ. Once this covenant has been established through the shed blood of Jesus Christ, no one can disclaim your state of repentance or forgiveness of sins, simply because you are not in alignment with their scope of thinking or religious ideologies. Being saved and receiving this newness in Christ, is not something that man can determine, no matter their opinions and critique of your past. You are saved by grace (God's unmerited favour, *Ephesians 2:8-9*). Salvation is from God and God alone, no one else. He's the final Judge over your life.

As a matter of fact, our flesh will always be the physical suit we wear day after day, even though at times I wish I could take it off somehow. It will constantly be the reckoning nature that will try us until the end. We cannot escape living in this garment and having to fight its daily desires. They are never going to give us an easy chance of survival. Why? Because it is the initial doorway through which sin was introduced and our functioning abilities coincide with it, whether we like it or not. It's how we were made and our inherited genes for sin were sown through Adam and Eve's disobedience. You may say, "Why is it so hard to live in this manner and why aren't we able to get rid of sin?" Honey, I have wondered the same thing for years and you know what I found out, my flesh is with me everyday I'm awake. We have to accept that this is what we have inherited as our covering in order to live

[69]

on earth. God suited us up as such and it is only in Him that we are able to endure whatever sufferings may come our way. Listen! Sin does not have to dictate your life or reduce you to a limited vision of you. You have the power to reign over sin, to have dominion over it and rule your life effectively through grace. Sin will only live, if you permit it to do so!! Honey, the last thing you'll wish to do is to sit in a sin conscious state and devalue your humanity or lessen your life to a sin restricted life. Sin as it is, and while it will be what it is, you do not have to let its sting of death or the shadows of its reign constrict your humanity into any unlawful premise of existence. Lady! You have the power to subdue and put sin where it belongs, under the blood of Jesus.

Naturally, it is easy to say live in the flesh, meaning, do whatever you feel, think and want without God's operation in your life but that will only result in your spiritual death and eternal separation from God. Certainly, this is not the road I wish for you to travel and neither would I sit here and lie to you concerning your position. What I will request of you, is to take the bit of strength you have on the inside and strive to walk as God requires. In this way, your life will bear much fruit. Walking in this new found state will be a challenge for you but it is not impossible. Once you are open and willing to appropriate God's mercies daily, while seeking to honour Him with your all, He will aid you with His Spirit, so that you will know He's with you to the end. Furthermore, He will make sure that your course of life finds new meaning through His love. I can guarantee that you will reap a harvest of living so much richer than before, that it will cause your soul to drink more and more. With this humble invitation, please take my hand and let us open the sacred pages of life, to see God's infinite portrait of the image called *WOMAN*.

At the very beginning, when Eve was created, God brought her to Adam. Interestingly, notice here that Adam had no clue as to what God was up to on his behalf, until God presented him with the gift called *'Woman'*. On seeing this creature for the first time, he was stumped, totally in awe, and the captivating figure blew his mind away. God, as creator, gives to Adam, a well built complete and groomed physique made from his rib, of a type equal to him. The rib in essence, signifies a connection that was in no way intended for either Adam or Eve to survive on their own merit. Instead, it was composed of a unifying cord with an eternal bond.

Eve, in her own capacity as a woman, had a sense of creativity that was not limited, yet not having the absolute power to stand alone, in the same way Adam could not remain alone. Their divine construct, intent and purpose mirrored oneness. Having fallen from this fixated state of being, they both bore the mark of a significant spiritual disconnection, which shattered God's creative ideal and genetic artistry. Furthermore, the twist that came and brought about chaos was that one evening Eve decided to wander on her own, walking about in the cool of the day. With an already established habitat, there was little work for Eve to do, so getting acquainted with her environment seems to be just the right taste of pleasure. As she walked, her interest focused on examining all the fruits, trying to make up her mind which one to eat, until she saw one that caught her attention fully. While the story that unfolded after her curiosity has much relevance, my aim is geared towards engaging your scope of thinking more in relation to her introduction in creation. An area I believe needs serious consideration if we are going to see the wealth and merit in the artistry of woman through God's eye.

Ladies, hear me well, your design was never a counterfeit, but a masterpiece, in my opinion, that never got the full opportunity to be marketed into the magnitude of its glory. We cannot afford to let the degradation of society eat away at our excellence and essence. Ladies! We are worth more than THIS. Get the picture clear in your minds! You were brought from space and time to perfect the intent of God's connective balance equation and to express the unity that coincides with His heart, mind and Spirit. Ladies, let us not divert from the Genesis model to settle for less in comparison to what God knows, far better than the norm of our cultures and the world's perception. God made sure to give us a habitation with a wealth of provision that had both physical and spiritual substance and longevity eternally. Let us get this clear women, God was the one who provided this milieu without the help of man or woman and He chose to accredit this foundation to mankind. Get it right! Ladies, God afforded you this well deserved blessing. And I believe, at this point, that all the women who are reading this should jump from their seats and start singing, Glory, Hallelujah!

Can you permit me to bring this home, with a greater sense of understanding, so that you will not miss a single thought? First, God being our Father took the pleasure to establish creation filled with all we need for our natural and spiritual survival. Then, He made man to take charge over this said creation so that it would be maintained as long as he lived on earth. He was so genuine at heart to even let Adam in on the action by giving him the opportunity to name the animals. Eve was not formed as yet. Have you noticed that so far, it was only Adam? Yet God knew the sadness that would have overwhelmed Adam's heart had He left him alone. His incompleteness would have surely been spotted afar off and this may have caused him to get bored quite often with just creation as his companion. Hmmm! I figured Adam would have one day approached God himself and asked for something to connect to like himself, poor man with no one *(companion)* to talk to but the animals. Lol! Oh my...

Interestingly, God in all His splendor and wisdom had an incentive to bring Adam at a place where he could enjoy himself and feel comfortable in his own environment. So, He put Adam's head to rest from all the stress of living alone. God took the matter at hand and began a surgery that the world's doctors will never be able to perform. At last the scales of sleep fell from Adam's eyes, something was not right. He felt strange, but whole. As he stood to his feet, amazingly his face came aglow with a rush of excitement that crippled his knees and ankles with such weakness that caused his heart to palpitate. Before his face, was God and someone familiar but suddenly felt close, filling the void and the absence he felt for so long. He waited with patience as God took hold of the creature's hand and placed it in his own, pronouncing a union that knitted, mind, soul, spirit and body; a oneness that exceeds all of earth's boundaries. He was finally complete, finally one, finally engaged in union, finally intertwined and interlocked beyond words.

He was no longer naming animals as a hobby and neither was he sight seeing nature's finest environ but was now wrapped in a moment of seclusion, while his nostrils inhaled the beauty before him. This is now bone of my bone and flesh of my flesh *(Genesis 2: 22-23)*. Adam's sixth sense kicked in with such sharp gear beckoning his 20-20 vision to hold this image secure, lest his internal imbalance crumbled into a comical motion. He was so fixated that his language expressed the final tone of God's intentions toward their new found companionship. They were sealed as one, even though they were apart and his rib would always represent that magnetic lock-combination which will give God the right to undergird their lives eternally.

On a serious note, how many of us women ever took the time to seriously observe our physique in the mirror - Every curve, every line, the unique texture, sculpture, tone, and composition? Have you ever tried understanding the way we're able to change our appearance so fashionably and not lose our nature? I'm always amazed at how we can do this; decorating ourselves with fashionable hairstyles, dresses, heels, bags, and so much more. But the funny thing is, we tend to have the ability to keep our composure and the texture of our design intact without any real depletion. Why am I saying this? When the first woman came into being, although we may not have had a physical picture of her, looking at a woman today can give us some means of insight into the beauty that was formed.

Seldom do we as women bring ourselves to a place of seeing the real picture that God intended. It's not about manipulating our position or losing the essentials over what we've cheapened ourselves to become; but it's simply about appropriating our design in the purest sense of the term, *Woman*. Eve came into a world already prepared for her entry without having to frustrate herself over the least inconvenient details of the day. She knew her position and humbly exercised it, in its fullest place. She did not resist the unique and natural gift built innately in her. She accepted who she was created to be, without any hesitation, in order to function as a pure woman in her complete form. Her grace as a woman filtered through Adam's heart at first glance. She didn't have to fight, quarrel, argue, or show who was boss much less fit into any masculine tone to prove her womanhood. She freely lived in her creative form and made life worthwhile through the eternal value God placed on her femininity. Ladies! Can we truly get into the pureness of the woman we were made to be. This is the most incredible essence of who we are, in *SPIRIT.*

Please do not mistake this discovery as a cover up for Eve's sin and the repercussions we are now facing. You will have to understand that before Eve ventured out to eat the fruit; she was first created as a woman in her full right. There was no falsehood in her nature and neither was her demeanor compromised in any form. She was truly woman in character and her personality reflected the feminine imprints of God's intent. Yes, she was without sin and innocent to the likes of it all. As a matter of fact, it was God who personified Himself through the image and likeness of what Eve was created as; or permit me to say that God took a piece of Himself and added the finale to Eve's perfect outlook. No arguments here! It was God who made her from Adam's rib and brought her to him. So Adam had no clue how she was made and how God performed His works on her to bring her into what He saw. I guess Adam enjoyed the easiest part of the job, which is to receive her with all honour.

I'll reinforce one thing here for the many ladies who may assume that regaining this place in God is a mistake and a waste of good old time. Women who may perceive in their minds that it is no use and may think that we are too far gone from Eve's day. You were created in the image and likeness of God, not man, not the world, not society, not your family, not even the job you're in or your husband. No one created you to be you, more than God and certainly as Eve lived in the woman's nature in which she was created, so can you. Let me assure you of this important key note, the nature within you cannot change or be altered for something else. You are a woman and that is what you will be until you die, there are no two ways about it.

I know that the thoughts of those so-called superiors (*the psychologists, scientists, plastic and sex-change surgeons, etc*) may tend to pervert your minds into thinking that you can change your sex organs or any part of you to be what you want to be. If you are caught in this web, for one reason or the other, you are only hurting yourself and denying the divine order of your creation. You cannot and will never change what you already are by nature. No amount of surgery, sex-change or adaptive attitudes, behavioural patterns and duplication of any sort will diminish what God built. Hey lady!! Fact check, you are an eternal replica. No one can duplicate or manipulate creation. You cannot create BREATH or LIFE!! All you are doing is violating your natural order for what seems good to you, which is temporary and leads to eternal death *(Romans 1:18-32)*. For those of you who may have suffered any such sexual trauma, there is hope for you, once Christ becomes a part of you. Change is unlimited with God, surely He can make all things new *(2 Cor.5:17)*.

The reality is that these narrow minded beliefs and myths are the devil's crafty pursuits to demolish your divine nature into what you believe is right for you. When this is allowed, you are no longer catering for the divine order in your life. It's a matter of what seems right and if it feels right, then just do it. The devil does not consider what you do as long as he causes you to believe that what you are doing is right and that is enough rope to hang yourself. Now I do not wish to go into full details about the carnal nature and its atrocious mentality but my humble plea is for us not to be deceived. You are uniquely *'You'* without any carbon copy or duplication. I am not too concerned about how far you have gone into sin, not that I am not mindful of your state and your need for change, but the real issue is for you to recognize that hope is available through Christ.

You may sit in your corner and wonder how am I able to understand when I am not the one in your position. I will say this to you, I was there. There is a force that is greater than you, and although you may very well wish to come out from where you are, you cannot do it alone, not without God's helping hand. Eve messed up what God wanted us to enjoy and there is no way that we can change the damage done by ourselves. As one of my friends indicated to me when I was in great distress, *"You cannot put back the milk in the cow, it's already spilled. You either leave it there or you clean it up."* God provided even before Eve sinned and though this aspect of our lives resulted in so much controversy, we are still without excuse if we fail to accept His standard for change. He afforded us salvation through His Son Jesus Christ so what we lost in the beginning can be restored in full.

Failing to see you through the eyes of God, knowing He made you will only bring confusion and mental turmoil because your efforts to make you better will not suffice. This is where your own merits for survival cannot compensate for God's order. What Eve had going for her was the ideal spirituality that was consummated through God's image and likeness. She was not just flesh and blood, but Spirit. She understood where her real livelihood was centered. It was embedded innately through the feminine spirit who knew where to unlock the door to find refuge and strength in the most painful hour.

In spite of the error committed, from her eating of the fruit, God switched the fate for the enemy by using the woman's seed to crush his head. In all truth, Eve was responsible for her shortcomings but God through Eve's sin used the opportunity to unleash His power to repay the enemy for his deception. What a God! The devil's payment for sin and his deception came through the very woman he deceived. Imagine, God used the same woman's seed to nullify the devil's counteraction of His creation *(Genesis 3:15)*.

Therefore, in as much as God restored Eve from her fallen state so too can you be restored from where you are. Restoration is possible!! You may look at Eve and wonder how a flawless woman could be led so stupidly and I guess she would say no less of herself but neither was she exempted from turning back to God's original state. In spite of being the first woman made, she too fell and had to suffer the consequences just like all of us who follow our own ways and not God's *(Proverb 16:25)*.

Furthermore, it is not until we appropriate God's salvation in our lives, that we can find the grace to live as God desires. No matter the depletion of our lives and how far sin's ruin can be traced, it is only the blood of Jesus Christ that can emanate new life in its truest form. Eve may have lost it and fallen for the deception of the serpent in the Garden but it did not stop her from being the woman she was designed to be. The enemy thought he had control of God's plan but he lost even at Eve's hand, in the end *(Genesis 3:15)*.

Ladies, we are all God's precious blueprint and amidst our struggles or pains, God's eyes are never short sighted about who we are in Him. We are the ones who lose sight, especially when we cause ourselves to believe that we could make it on our own. It is high time for us to see ourselves as God sees us, rather than just being satisfied with what we think we are or can be. It is only then that we are going to win the war internally. When we see ourselves in God's eyes, there are no limits to what we can become and what we can do. God knows the power He invests in us and it's about time that we learn to recapture that innate power that almost knocked Adam down when he first saw Eve. She didn't say a word and the man went off babbling ahead of himself. Can we give God the freedom to make us whole again?

Women, when God sees you, He sees a woman of divine vestry, virtue, value, worth, essence, charisma, beauty, excellence, power, majesty, royalty and grace because that is what He invested in you beforehand. He sees that you are able to crawl out from where you are and get back up to the whole and refined image situated on the internal circumference of your being. Eve bounced back and so can you. She remained in the totality of her nature amidst the plight of deception. Amidst the branded scar of sin written all over her pages! Amidst the soil in her clothing- the garment she had to wear night and day through the hardship of life outside Eden. She stood the test and kept destruction at bay. You are a woman and certainly God sees you as no less. So take off the scales from your eyes and let him help you to see yourself in Him, whole and complete.

So why not allow yourself the privilege of stepping out to become the woman you have always longed to be. Face the mirror, face the music before you and if what you see is not what you want to be, then start allowing God to see you through His eyes. He will surely fulfill the job He started in you and bring you back to his original design. Open your eyes and look beyond your limited perception. God is able to do what He knows is best for you. Tap into Him today and you will see the difference He'll make when you see Him as He sees you.

Chapter 7

'Let's be Real'

Being real will call for your submission to God in full, no matter the condition of your heart and how far you've gone. Sin is not an impossible act that cannot be forgiven.

I can imagine the reflective state of mind that you are in presently and the challenge at hand to review your status, both internally and externally. Yet, I cannot refrain from treating this chapter outside of being real and completely honest with you. Ladies! No, I am not being insensitive or hard on anyone, at all. And if in any way I come across to you as such, kindly know that it is with every intent to see the good. There's a deep measure of concern that is like a burden in my spirit for women who misplace their identity, value and worth. Even those who clothe themselves in the arms of the church whether they are in the choir, worship team, administrative department or the pulpit. There are those with self righteous mindsets, religious garments, pious esteem as if they rule with this subtle sense of conceit, who believe that they will be comforted with what religion offers. I'm also referring to those who hide themselves in the closet, in premature and unhealthy marriages, those with husbands who do not belong to them, parading themselves in idle conduct that kills the very atmosphere in the house of God. Not just those on the outskirts of the world who are bruised and battered, but those of us who tend to think God's eyes are closed from the folly we create, while thinking that our gifts and graces can save us from the consequences of our actions. Women! Let us stop fooling ourselves, sin is sin. It has no colour, size and obviously it has no favourite side. It settles where it is freely accommodated. So let's get the picture as clear as crystal. Let's be real.

I do not know how you feel when you see a woman televised as a rape victim, abused by several men, in such a heinous manner that leaves her broken and void. I mean it's almost intolerable to go through life after such a hideous act. Yet God's grace abounds in ways that I am still learning to grasp. On the hand, there are those who voluntarily violate their beings and cheapen themselves to such an extent that had it not been for grace, I have no idea how they would be saved. Now ladies, do not get me wrong here, but we have not always been easy to deal with. I believe God is saying to us that we need to take a spiritual check up and clean up ourselves from all this mess we've created. While there are those who fell into the lion's den and became victims innocently, there are those who simply navigated their own course into some wild zones that left such a stench that we have to cover our noses. I am not going to sit here and pretend that we haven't failed big time in being who we are as women. We have to stop blaming the men too, and start owning our wrongs.

To top it off, we enjoy the whole blame game and sometimes make men appear to be the worst creatures God ever put on the earth to live among us. I think we need to look closer and see that we are a part of the whole game. So you can say the game is on us too, not just the men. What happens most of the time is that we hate to accept the truth and let that truth ultimately lead to change. We quench every time when we're caught red handed and the easiest thing is to cast the blame on *'Adam'*. My question is, when are we going to grow up and learn to act responsibly? When are we going to sit in a seat of accountability and be credible to ourselves?

As blatant as this may sound, I think we have gravitated towards some serious consequences over our destiny. In other words, we will be responsible for the things we allow to impact our lives, especially when they are not the right condiments for our soul and spirit. Oftentimes we find it so easy to cheat, lie, steal, or even fornicate. But when it comes to doing what is right, we grimace and would look for an excuse just so that we can gain ground for our unhealthy practices. Hmmm, I could never imagine living in a closet like this forever. I mean, I'll suffocate to death with all these unhealthy medications for my spirit. Come on now ladies, I can almost see you trying to dodge the truth here.

You may say, *"That's easy for you to say Sheldene",* but the truth is, there will not be any real satisfaction for the soul if you choose to remain in this den. I think what a lot of us women are fearful of is facing the reality of our issues because we prefer to cover up our faults just like those we watch on lifetime TV. Surely, Wendy Williams and Oprah Winfrey do not have the answers. Only God does! Of course, we would wish to argue this case further but we need to be mindful that repercussions will always be harder to face and wanting an easy way out is the natural inclination. What often causes my eyebrows to rise are those dreadful misrepresentations that we echo in society, making the world more chaotic than ever. We've gone so far in wanting our own way that we are now running a movement that seeks to fight for our rights as women. Yes! I am referring to the liberation movement for women rights *(the feminist movement).* This is truly amazing. Yet I have one question to ask, why would you fight for a right that naturally belongs to you? In my opinion, you will only do so when you give up that

[83]

right freely to someone else. And when you realize that it's been manipulated into something else, you go about screaming for its return.

From my point of view, I believe that this movement is a sexist trap syndrome, call me old fashioned, but I honestly think that the motives behind these women's voices are misleading. Let me affirm this to you directly, your right has been afforded to you divinely, certainly not by man's dictation. Therefore, there is no need to fight for what is already yours. It would appear as if these women sought an open door to provide a forum for the many voices of error to be heard, and granted they did so with a sense of right. However, their actions speak to a means to an end and they have taken a route that has left many still wishing to find true freedom; a freedom that cannot be attained through mere human efforts. I applaud these women for trying but the battle is too big for us to recover our true nature on our own. All we have really done is cheapened our original context into a *'battle of the sexes'*.

I will simply say this; because I believe this is the crucial point we've missed over the years. **"When we choose to give up our rights as women, we are giving the privilege to another to have full *'rule or reign'* over us without charge."** Mind you, when I speak of rights here, I am not referring to that heady mindset where *"women run things"* becomes the practice. I am referring to what God innately gives to us, that is, our nature, our being, our creation, essence, joy, peace, integrity, and wisdom. We are the ones who got caught, hook, line and sinker for being so carefree with what should have been our prized possession and living abundantly. No wonder Eve's mistake in Genesis Chapter 3 demonstrates for us the resounding theme of idiocy in search of absolute power. This will surely lead us into temptation, of which we may not even know the way out. Beware of this quote; ***"The quest for absolute power is the recipe for havoc in disguise."*** It is a quotation that I coined after reading about Eve's dilemma and I would hope it sensitizes your mind from such selfish ambitions.

If we keep fighting and exhausting ourselves in this ploy for making our stand, we will only end up doing it over and over again. To see the irony in this, let us picture a group of women shouting to the world and announcing through every doorway, *"We want our rights back, we want to be women, we want our freedom back, we want the world to know that we are women and we deserve to be women."* Can you imagine what we are really saying here? Can you see how foolish our poor attempts are? All we are doing is saying to the world give us back our rights as women, while parading the streets without understanding our failures, without addressing the core or root of our folly. And we are literally begging the world for what they cannot give.

Have you ever noticed that whenever there is a protest, even though it may stir concerns or raise eyebrows, the final outcome is still in the hands of those in authority? This goes to show that regardless of our shouting or mouthed expressions for our rights; we will never be able to achieve the definitive on our own merit. We must go back to the source whether we like it or not. There is no way we will win the war without knocking ourselves over, leaving our souls bleeding continuously. Ladies, we've got to understand that it is in God we've been created. It is He who made us and not we ourselves *(Ps. 100: 3)*. So no amount of protest or effort, on our terms, will bring us back into the position we have been given in the beginning unless we reclaim our heritage in Jesus Christ. Have you forgotten that we were called *'Woman'* in the Garden of Eden? That's who we are inside- Out! For example, if you take a mouse and take the skin off, does it change the nature of the mouse? You will still get a mouse. Your nature is divine, of the Spirit of God, not merely natural.

Lovely ladies, it is critical for us to untangle ourselves from all the fuss and tension of trying to be a woman, on our own terms and conditions, without any regard for the divine order. We may have come from all walks of life and may have succumbed to various forms of sin which proved to be costly in the end but hope is still in existence. It would not be fitting of me to tell you that you can go about your own affairs and live on a cloud all your life without falling. What many of us refrain from in life is the whole issue of humility and honesty. We prefer to put on the gloves, and stand in the ring, ready to take on the champions who believe they can *'rule'* over us.

You may sit there on your sofa and prop up your shoulders or laugh and say, *"Ain't nobody gonna rule over me, hell no! Are you crazy, ain't nobody getting such power over me, you gotta be kidding me."* Now, before you crucify me, let's take what I am saying in moderation. First of all, if we are entirely honest with ourselves, we will not deny our share in the whole blame game affair. In fact, Eve was the initiator for sin's entrance into our lives and by extension the world. I will suggest that you take a good look and understand that neither of us as human beings can run away from something that we caused. And it would have been wise on Adam and Eve part to simply admit their wrongs instead of stirring a deeper controversial debate that we are now experiencing.

Women!! What we are running from is the confrontation of our own wrongs. I am not in any way exempting the man in all of this; I wished that Adam had used his senses instead of just freely accepting Eve's offering of the fruit without question. I wish that Adam had reminded Eve of the instruction given by God, so that they would have been kept in divine safety. At least, we may have received an easier sentence than the one we were given so sternly. Nevertheless, my emphasis here is not to make it appear any easier for either person, failing to realize our responsibility in the act shared. Rather, it's a matter of helping Adam and Eve to stop running. Yes, that is, you and me.

Let's face it; our world is already messed up in every way we can imagine. We are responsible for where it is today, full stop!! Going about our business daily with the blame game and sexist battle will not resolve anything. It will only compound our shortcomings, more and more. Are you not downright tired of seeing our homes, families, workplaces, and churches filled with such chaotic scenarios, while our livelihood suffers silently? I honestly believe that all of this stems from one single word that God spoke over Eve's sin as a judgment for the rest of her life and that word is *'Rule'*. There is no doubt that Eve was caught red handed and one of the consequences for man to rule was the natural part of her punishment *(Genesis 3:15-16)*. So she had to face the mirror and accept this pronouncement no matter how she felt. She knew she had done wrong and that God was the authoritative personnel to direct His course of action against their wrong deed. There was no escape and she simply had to allow God to govern His creation at best. She didn't even try to put up a defense mechanism after her total surrender in the matter.

Tell me, why would we want to hide ourselves from coming to terms with our own error even when we are caught by God Himself? Are we aware of the implications if we fail to surrender and correct our ways? I do not believe we are able to handle the outcome of such impetuous actions and neither would we be able to stand against God with any sort of *'guilt trip'* game. It's pointless! So I will suggest, no arguments, simply admit your wrong and whatever may come with it lest you suffer far more than you can bear. Believe me, it's not worth fighting with yourself, much less fight with God. You will *NOT* win!!

In so far as Eve suffered the loss of Eden's well prepared habitation and was banished from her majestic paradise, she still did not lose sight of her internal nature. Despite the curse handed down to her and the separation that came with it- *that disconnection from divine fellowship with the King-* she came around to understanding the need for obedience rather than following her own way. Notice, after God spoke, afterward Eve was silent and humbled herself by following His directives because she knew that there was no need to argue with God. It was her just reward for disobedience and she accepted her fate in spite of the hardship that came with it.

God, on the other hand, was so sensitive to Eve's spirit that He made firsthand provision for her to rekindle that sacred part of their union so that her life would not be void of His presence forever. He knew that she would need His aid and He did not resist supporting her in full. She realized that she was incapable of cleansing the mess she had made by any righteous doing of her own. It was only able to be restored by the One whose true authority she had displeased and she had to yield to His way rather than messing up again. Eve simply subjected herself to God anew and God in return forgave her with a cleansing that was now able to help her survive in her new environment.

I can remember the day when I was forgiven of the sins I committed. At first, I used to feel as if I really didn't deserve this opportunity because in my mind I didn't do anything to clean up my acts of sin. I felt so lame, in the sense that I could do nothing to change my state much less remove the sin on my own terms. It was not until I accepted the whole idea of God's love for me that I understood His grace and pardon from sin. I used to think that God was not responsible for the sin that I committed and neither should He clean me up. I did it, so it was my mess to clean, not His.

Actually I was wrong, for the most part, there was nothing I could do to clean away the sins committed and I had to freely accept God's pardon so that His grace could saturate my heart to make a fresh start. This is the reason why we all need to bow at His feet and clothe ourselves in His grace and mercy in order to see ourselves anew in Him. In our efforts to redeem ourselves, we fail miserably and we will never accomplish the works God concluded on Calvary on our own behalf. We can only reenter Eden under His terms and conditions, not what we perceive to work in our eyes.

No wonder we are afraid to be real with ourselves and God. Why? Because we dislike the idea of being naked and exposed. We hardly admit our faults, wrongs, errors, dishonesty, lies, and failures. It is only until we surrender or yield then God can grant us pardon without any hesitation. David, the Psalmist is an ideal example for us here *(2 Samuel chapter 11 & Psalm 51).* I cannot think of a better man to fit this scenario so figuratively Ohhh!!! He had such a heart for God and would have done what it takes to make sure that he remained penitent before Him. In all of David's actions, he never resisted the need for God in his life. He never retaliated from correction, particularly when Nathan approached him with God's judgment, and neither did he ever behave self righteously, unlike Saul, who stood on his own feet apart from God. David understood that it was only in God that his salvation was affirmed, not in himself or man.

Can I stick a pin here for a few minutes and take this idea about Eve's judgment a bit further? Let's look at something here closely. When her actions were found out by God, Adam didn't even think of defending her by admitting that they both had disobeyed. Look at what he said, *"The woman whom you give to be with me, she give me of the tree, and I ate"* (Genesis 3:12), which showed that he had lost the whole concept of his responsibility as a husband much less the understanding of his portfolio as the man. He didn't cover her when she was broken and neither did he venture to act as the head over her as a wife. Hmmm!!!! Adam figured that it was easier to blame God because it was He who gave Eve as his wife. My world!! Perhaps, Adam reacted in that way because he had stayed with the animals a bit too long and forgot that his mentality had to change when it came to his wife. In fact, his priorities were mixed up. After all, he was caught just like Eve and wanted an easy way out of the whole situation because he could not deal with his failure.

Permit me to say here, had Adam realized his position and responsibility before God and his wife, things may have had an easier twist but he failed to represent God and his wife. So it is not fair to encourage this whole

[90]

blame game affair. Let's abandon it right here because we both lost it in the beginning. We both lost our sense of honour towards God and ourselves right there in the garden. We were given freedom beyond any human language and we destroyed it on our own terms. We were irresponsible and failed to manage as God required of us. In fact, we both received the command to have dominion over the earth *(Genesis 1:28-29)*. This was not a matter of competition; we were equal in God's eyes in spite of our physical differences.

The worst part in this drama, as to why we women fail to be real and open before God, is that we cannot control our sense of pride and ego. Eat my head off if you can, but answer me this simple question, what transpired when Eve came into the picture? In her flawlessness she went ahead feeling so giddy headed, she wandered off. I guess she was way too caught up in her own world that she paraded with all her innocence, flaunting it so much that her beauty attracted the wrong eye. She had no idea as to what was ahead of her without God's intervention and redemption.

May I say something here ladies. When we act in such a manner and fail to capitalize on God's protection we will always suffer the consequences. Regardless, whether you're married or not, you cannot and should not, under any given circumstances, deter from God's divine coverage and wander off without your rightful guard. The devil will eat you raw! You are too fragile to be left unprotected and you are more receptive and susceptible to temptations. So, be careful about your strength, especially when you try flexing your muscles like a man. Use your womanhood carefully. Why am I saying this? It's simply because, too often we are clouded with our own ideals and supposed theories about not needing the protection, care, shielding, guarding and safety of God, and yes a man/ husband. We cannot be so foolish to think that we have it made for ourselves and go around with that kind of hypocritical thinking. We are seriously out of line ladies. God's creation is clear, not twisted and we need each other, no matter what. We are created to function in God as one, submissive to each other under His order, not as separate entities.

At one point in my life, I was guilty of this misconception. I was in Bible College when I got engaged in a conversation with one of my colleagues about the whole concept surrounding submission. I'm aware that this is a scary or offensive term to some of us women, but please hold on for a second here. Don't be too quick to jump to conclusions without first getting the facts right. I remembered saying to him that I would never be submissive to a man, no way, never, because of all the dominance, rule and subordination existing around me. I hated to think that such a man could have me in any relationship whatsoever, and mind you, I was still going through my healing process. It was not until I fully came to understand my relationship with God that my perception took a different turn. As a matter of fact, submission has nothing to do with inferiority versus superiority nor dominance versus control. Submission is simply an attitude or act of the heart that is voluntarily offered to another in service. It has nothing to do with all the myths and vain thoughts we're accustomed to hearing. Ladies, let's drop the whole attitude of trying to rule our own destiny. Our destinies are not without God's predestined mind towards us, and it is certainly not a controlled theory by our human intentions.

The curse in itself, that which was principally handed down to Eve, was reflective of her efforts to *"be in charge of her own destiny"*. Everything took a different turn and resulted in her punishment. Her God-given connection, that embodiment of God's Spirit dwelling securely on the inside was ripped apart. Her desires were now offered to Adam, since she failed to show honour to God in His rightful respect. Adam was now the object of *'rule'* over such desires and she would always be in a position of trying to satisfy this need within her soul.

Moreover, Eve's rebellion was now transferred into a mode of control that Adam would infect her spirit with, all through her life *(she would be seeking for her own sense of power while he would be seeking for ruler-ship and control)*, since she wrenched her arms away from the one who ignited this savored reservoir for Himself. She refused to be cuddled in a womb of freedom where her worship need not be compromised but instead took a bite of an opportunity that wrecked her world from enjoying her shared companionship in its full proportion and splendour. How was Eve so careless to fall for a lousy trap like that, you may ask? But anyone of us can be faulted in the same manner, no wonder we need God's reinstallation more than anything else.

What a tragedy? Wow!! Ladies, can you imagine the extent of the damage done! We are now left with a challenge, that will either make us or break us, and we dare not think that we can do it without God. We need Him more than ever to help us combat the enemy's snare against the rest of our fragmented lives because He is the only one who can reinstate all that was savaged. I will say this for the single ladies, you are not the master of your own destiny, so do not wander off in life without having God at the very foundation. Do not go about fooling yourselves with all the classified wisdom of the world that you've inherited and think that you do not need God to cover your lives. It would be a total disaster if you sink yourself into your own world of deceit. No amount of luxury from the world is viable enough to save your soul, and to save you, without the acknowledgement of God in your lives. Eve's example is enough for you to get the picture.

Having opened your eyes to see the need to be real, in the sense of becoming naked and unashamed before God; you will now have to take the courage to let go and let God in, on everything, since your newness would have to be redeemed through Him. Walking out of Eden, for both parties, was a heartrending experience, yet God made sure that He took charge and gave them another opportunity to correct their fallen state. This is why I made mention of David earlier and brought about an understanding that would help you to see the need for remaining penitent and in adherence to God's directive. You cannot be real and wish to dominate, rule, dictate, or govern your own affairs with the thought of making life as you deem best. It is a diabolic set up for your eternal downfall. Being real will call for your submission to God in full, no matter the condition of your heart and how far you've gone. Sin is not an impossible act that cannot be forgiven.

David demonstrated his heart in a way that revealed his love for God beyond his failures. No wonder God referred to him as a man after His own heart. We need to align ourselves in like manner, for a broken and a contrite heart is what God would not despise *(Psalm 51:17)*. God is full of compassion and His bowels of mercy are forever filled to capacity. And you need not think that you have to stay away from God's presence and neglect your opportunity to become transparent before His face.

It is only when you open up that He will in turn pour Himself on you, giving you that extra push to see the beauty He created in you. Lift up your heads from shame and guilt and from the enemy's scope of deception. See yourself as a vessel that God is willing to fill with all the necessary contents to keep you functioning as a well established source for his purpose and intent in the world. Give yourself a chance to experience God afresh, as well as, your womanhood. His mercies are indeed new every morning. Let go, be real before His presence. Take off the mask that you have worn for years. Come naked, no pretense, no polish, and no procrastination, just be real without any added embellishments and let Him take you to new heights in His love. You'll be astounded by what transformation can do to your whole life when God is seated on the throne of your heart. Sis! You have the power to be a whole woman.

Chapter 8

'The Forgiveness Issue'

Forgiveness literally is the key ingredient that connects and sustains healing, to the point where restoration is fulfilled. One cannot find true healing unless forgiveness is initiated. In essence, this act breaks down every barrier that sin seeks to penetrate.

This is one aspect of life that I've wondered about and pondered on for years. I tried in many ways to determine how this little word, *'Forgive'* proves to be so mind boggling, complex and why many of us struggle to even realize, actualize or practice this said principle. I've heard the relentless notion over and over again, *"It's easier said than done."* The ironic twist is when a person who expresses this same phrase, stands in the position of needing forgiveness, receives forgiveness, and then turns around refusing to forgive another. Interestingly, it is a common act that many of us run from doing, even in the Kingdom of God.

Here is a thoughtful question, what happens to the person who is in need of forgiveness from the same person who applied the notion above? Doesn't that same person who was refused forgiveness need to be forgiven? Hmmm! Although some of us may be tempted to see this as a controversial issue, it is imperative for us to view this as God indicates. More so, if we are citizens of God's kingdom then forgiveness is mandatory. No bars hold! The realistic outlook is that many of us fail to deal with this issue of unforgiveness and instead allow it to fester for years and form blockages that hardens our heart. Instead of understanding the need for a person to be forgiven we refuse and therefore stifle our own growth in Christ.

Frankly speaking, what right do you have to be forgiven, if you fail to forgive? I can almost see some of your eyes popping and your shoulders shifting, with a questioning look, perhaps even wondering what am I really saying. The objective here is not about taking sides or easing any one's hypocritical mindset, much less filing a justification report that suits your uncircumcised hearts. You may be tempted to close the book right at this point since within your perception I'm harsh or unsympathetic. Yet the truth remains! Ladies, I'm not accusing anyone here at all, but at times we have to face the reality of our actions and thoughts, even our ignorance and self righteousness. For decades upon decades we have suffered relentlessly because of this issue with unforgiveness and we fail to see how much damage is being piled up beneath the carpet of our lives. Truth be told, we cannot move on, function, operate or live spiritually healthy lives with unforgiveness. It is a cancer to the soul!

No wonder God cannot find room to dwell in hearts that are so filthy! Hearts, with residues of unforgiveness, that have been nursed continually! And if we are truthful we will start to see just what a mess we have made not just in our own lives but also in the lives of others we refuse to forgive. In fact, we wrestle with forgiving ourselves, husbands, children, mothers, fathers, brothers, sisters, friends, neighbours, and at times, God Himself. Why? Because our focus is so much on the hurt and pain caused that we hardly ever stop to see our reflection in Christ when we disobey His laws. We are no less of an offender to others and ourselves. You and I were part of the equation in the first place!!

Let me be a bit more practical here by asking a simple question. How easy is it for you to forgive someone who has done you something really terrible? I mean something that you may not even dare to tell another person. Do you first sit and think about the hurt until your head aches at night? Or do you concoct plans that would bring harm to the person, curse in your minds, try to justify your point of view, go about angry all your days and just treat people indifferently because of what has happened? Or do you react with such a mannerism that dispels hate and even causes your life to be so bitter that the little life you have left in you suffocates and recedes daily? I believe we are guilty of at least one of these aspects mentioned.

Mind you, I am not trying to ignore the problem or rather the person who has done you wrong but instead I am trying to bring your mind to a place of understanding that this whole problem will be wreaking and creating havoc in your lives if you continue in this vein. Although you are the recipient of the hurt caused, do you know that the more you allow this hurt to fester the worse it becomes, and the more your life would be in misery? I can hear many of you shouting in my ears, but Sheldene, *"I am the one who was hurt, I didn't do the person anything, I'm the victim here, not you, so what are you really saying?"*

Oh! Ladies, ladies, take off the gloves please! Let us reason this out together, ok! May we kindly proceed in harmony without the yelling and shouting, please. Now, I'm not acting in a way to make you think that I'm without empathy for your situation, as some of us would have experienced pain in various forms. Yes! It hurts beyond measure when we are violated, mistreated, misjudged, harmed and branded with all sorts of wounds from life. Trust me, I've had my share! And I would not dare tell you that it was as easy as *'ABC'* to deal with the volume of pain buried. I understand that grievous moments can be awfully distressing to handle, but I would not wish to have you think that crossing over to freedom is unimaginable. It is absolutely possible in Christ!

One of the crucial things that we easily miss regarding forgiveness, is the understanding that the enemy plays his part in seeking to destroy our lives by any means or force (*1 Peter 5:8, St. John 10:10*). He does not need our approval to send attacks of all kinds, nor is he afraid to bombard our lives with anything that can eliminate us from earth. He will always be on our backs whether we like it or not. His mission is to liquidate our lives, if possible with every diabolic force from hell. Bless God! We have a defense that stands at our sides day and night to help us overcome, lest we succumb to the entire plight of the enemy's destructive devices. How easy it would be for us to become defenseless and hopeless without Christ! Remember the battle is not against flesh and blood. It is far more of a spiritual nature than our minds can envision *(Eph. 6:10-13)*.

Of course you go about life trying to live in peace and serve your communities as best as possible. No one should harm you for that and no one should try to destroy your life, not when you are doing all the good you can to advance and make others happy. Yet in the same manner, no one tells a perpetrator's mind that he should attack this person or that person except for the enemy's influence on his/her life. Take for instance the many women who are raped on a daily basis all over the world. These are women who suffer tremendously. I do feel pain for them, but the reality still stands. These victims are violated beyond words. This shows us that the enemy is the ultimate influential factor that entices the mind to promote such evil, why. Because of sin!

My sisters! No one likes to start their Monday mornings with such news surfacing the globe. It does something to our spirit and moves us to anger. If we are not careful, it may lead to retaliation of some detrimental nature. And what happens? Things only get worse and the life of the victim is still in need of restoration. We are well aware that the law exists and such perpetrators should be dealt with harshly. Trust me, some of us would go to the extreme without mercy. I once thought like that for some time but I've come to the realization that forgiveness has a greater power and value than adding injury to a man's soul. Seeing someone heading for hell is a scary sight to behold. I would not wish for my worst enemy to head in that direction. Getting to this point is hard, especially when you're looking at the offender and all the thoughts of the occurrence rises up on the inside of you. Surely you're tempted to do something there and then but that would only give the enemy more power over you. Remember, to whom you yield yourselves in obedience, that person or thing becomes your lord and then enslaves you to do their bidding.

In one way or the other, we are all at fault for failing to forgive as God requires, whether we admit it or not. While I will admit that in some instances forgiveness occurs progressively, there are times when we would have to consciously determine in our minds to forgive a person, no matter what was done. I believe we are familiar with this old saying, *"sometimes you have to give up your rights for peace sake"*. This is not a matter of being silly as some may think, but it has to do more with bringing your own sanity to a sense of freedom, rather than allowing the enemy to destroy your peace and finding the healing God alone can give.

Too often we clothe ourselves in the frame of mind that says we are not going to forgive since we are the ones who were hurt. If that is so, here is a question for you to ponder on, what transpires between two persons who would have had an argument over something that they were both guilty of but instead cast blame and aspersions? The only thing that I am seeing happening here are two guilty persons who fail to humble themselves, engulfed in their egos with no admittance to their errors while denying the choice to forgive each other. You would be amazed at some of the things people hold on to and go to their graves without forgiving. It is extremely sad.

Our biological and psychological makeup suffer immensely when we fail to let forgiveness reign. Some of the very folks who are lying in the hospitals are there on account of unforgiveness. Why? Believe it or not, they have become ill with the nursed issues and residues in their hearts that diseases find a home to live comfortably. A main problem that arises through these undealt traumas is *STRESS* which is caused by too much toxic waste in the mind and heart, with little or no room for purging. Why do we think it is so hard to forgive when we are commanded to forgive? Are we are not mindful that we are the ones who suffer the most when we live with unforgiveness?

How will healing be activated in us if we have hearts that are clogged with unforgiveness? Let me illustrate a picture for us here ladies. When Jesus Christ gave up His life on the cross, His blood was shed in each of our places for the remission of our sins. He did not think it too hard; neither did He refuse us a second opportunity to get things right with Him, because sin obviously could not have been atoned for by man in any way. It took an innocent person's blood to pay for humanity's ruthless and hideous acts of sin even though they ridiculed Him all the way to the cross. His blood was priceless. To be truthful, we didn't deserve this man's blood; we didn't even have to add to it, yet it was free of cost, no price tag attached.

Therefore, since Christ stepped in our place and forgave us freely even when we were guilty, as guilty can be, why then do we withhold forgiveness from someone else when it was not even our blood that was shed for that said person? You may wish to prove your point and justify your case on all accounts in your defense, but Christ was like a sheep led to the slaughter even by those who claimed to know God. How absurd was this! Yet, He hung there and asked His Father to forgive them for they know not what they do *(St. Luke 23:34).* The fact is, although the eyes of those who called for His death were blinded to the ultimate cause of freedom that would eventually be given to them, He chose to do it nonetheless, since they could not have saved themselves from their sins.

Do you know that the longer you shy away from forgiving someone, the more you lay waste to yourself in your own closet of misery? It is almost like you are sucked into a hole and you cannot find the freedom to live peacefully with yourself and others. The gospel is full of examples regarding this issue of forgiveness but one that captivates my mind is in relation to the woman who was caught in adultery *(St. John 8:1-11).* Now, I always ask this question, how many persons were involved in this act, why was only one person accused of the act and why were the Scribes and Pharisees so insistent on bringing the woman before Jesus to test His ability to Judge? Interesting, isn't it?

To the amazement of those who brought the woman to Jesus, with the hope that He was going to favour their decision, since Moses' law was still observed, Jesus swirled their thinking in another direction. He made this profound statement that baffled everyone's conscience, *"He who is without sin among you, let him throw the first stone at her".* (*St. John 8: 7)* I believe that Jesus in his wisdom struck the hammer right on the nail, leaving everyone to spiritually check their hearts instead of casting poor judgment, as well as condemnation. The hearts of the woman's accusers were by no means less than hers, since they realized sin was very much a part of their lives and they needed the same forgiveness, just as the woman. It is quite interesting how God can read our hearts, know our intentions and motives even before we can plead our cases before Him (*Jer. 17:9).*

So why do we disallow God the opportunity to work on our hearts and to bring us to a place where we can experience His healing touch of forgiveness? Are we not creating room for decay, knowing that God alone can forgive sins? I can use many illustrations from the Word of God to convince you of the need for appropriating forgiveness in your lives. However, if you fail to see that the healing you need is wrapped up in God alone, then it is null and void for me to even try. Ladies! To say the least, without allowing forgiveness to be cemented in your hearts, you will not be able to allow your spirit to find freedom in Christ blood; whereby you can be reconciled fully in his love and righteousness, far less to forgive others.

No amount of crying and self pity is going to get you to this point; no amount of closed doors to the issue is going to resolve anything. It is going to be there until you consciously decide to deal with it. Stop fooling yourselves by giving the enemy more room to harbor a dungeon in your soul. It's not worth it! As a matter of fact, only hurt would continually precede and compound your spiritual life from breathing the fresh air of healing you deserve. So who do you have in your closet that has been there for years that you haven't forgiven as yet? Who are you preventing from accessing the blood of Christ by your unforgiveness? Is it someone dear to your heart; a friend, husband, child, pastor, or is it you?

Think about it! Is it not easier for God to help you rather than fooling yourself into thinking that you can handle the job on your own terms and conditions? Why suffer yourself from being free and living at peace with God, the person or you? Eve certainly was glad when God restored her, knowing that she could have done nothing to undo the damage caused by her error. I bet she wished she could have held God back from announcing the curses He declared after He found out the horror of her actions. I would have really longed to take an exit flight out of Eden, if I were Eve. Hmmm, poor woman. She was left in total shame and disgust.

Imagine how sin rocks our world apart and leaves us as clueless victims with no way of fixing our errors on our own. Just imagine how the enemy laughs at us when we are totally broken and shattered. As long as he gets the job done through us, he's not even bothered by the results, much less the impact, except that it did him justice for his own cause. We are the ones who always get caught and misalign God's agenda for our lives. Yet God's mercies extends beyond the boundaries of the enemy's deception.

What I like about Eve's picture here, is the role God took to assure her of His forgiveness. On behalf of man, He was the first to demonstrate restoration, reconciliation and forgiveness. Look carefully at how God opened His heart and showed compassion to both parties for their irresponsible act. Despite the curse being handed down, He made sure to assure them afresh of His grace by clothing them with tunics made from an animal *(Gen. 3:21)*. This was the first sacrifice made, the very first restorative measure conducted on behalf of humanity. God literally restored mankind in the dignity and sanctity of His love.

Eve was reassured of her dignity in God again; in spite of having to live on the outskirts of Eden, in spite of having to wear a garment that was saturated by sin, in spite of having to live in the said garment and to face the penalty of its selfish nature. God made it possible to show Eve that her life in Him was more precious to save than affording the enemy a victory that he doesn't deserve, since life was His original creation and not the enemy's. The enemy was only trying to cheapen life to a place where he could intimidate and manipulate man's context of life. Yet he did not succeed in his intentions and motives, since God is the author of life. This is a secret that the enemy is still trying to unfold today. He still has no clue how to create life! What the enemy failed to come to grips with was that life was created in the image and likeness of God, and not in man himself. So trying to abort life from man's perspective was quite a tactful strategy on his part, but it did not suffice to win the war of life.

I firmly believe that the enemy will have to combat the author of life himself, if he wishes to find success. But how possible would that be for him? To sum it up, no attempt by the enemy to abolish life would ever be successful; no matter the strategy, the innovative efforts by the best intellectuals on earth. No, nothing, absolutely nothing!! Why? Because he cannot create life and all that we are seeing today as efforts are only copy *'cat'* attempts, mere duplication and replication that they would never ever attain fruition in the exact context as God. Are we not aware by now that man's ability is still limited and will never outmatch God's? *(Genesis Chapter 11)* So even though the enemy may use us as his instruments to thwart and retard God's creation, he will never fulfill his plans, no matter what he tries.

In fact, we are the only point of contact that the enemy has to use in order to try to interfere with God's creation, sad but true. Without us as his initial contact, he has no one and can use nothing else. He tried to deceive Eve in the garden into thinking that she could become like God *(Gen.3:1-5)* and certainly he is still promoting this faulty agenda among us in the world today. I firmly believe that the enemy forgot one major principle in God's creation when God made man and that is, a part of him has been invested in us. That is the breath of life He breathed into mankind, the ultimate ingredient that connects us to His- **His Spirit** *(Gen. 2:7 & St. John 4:24)*. Now tell me, how is it possible for the enemy to create breath again, something that he has absolutely no clue about and cannot create?

Therefore, how long will it take for us to understand that God is all omnipotent, omniscient, and omnipresent. He is all powerful and He is God and God alone. No one can ever be like Him much less to do what He can.

Remember, God was mindful to protect the '*Tree of Life*' in the garden and had all three persons dispatched out of Eden *(Gen. 3:22-24)*. He dealt with man's fall Himself!! As the creator, He understood His responsibility to man. And yes, it was through *MAN* that sin initially came into being, yet we seriously forget that God took action to preserve life because He is life. Right there in the garden, God mended and installed the very antidote to redeem and usher man back to Him. But the truth is we dwell on the nature of sin so much, that we scarcely take time to see God as our restorer and lose sight as to how He can restore us back to Eden.

Eve's nature (*her spirit*) was affected by sin but God provided her with the confidence to understand that He was still her reservoir, her identity, her primary source of life and more so her emblem of worship. Her essence in God was not diminished, neither was her spirit. The fact that God provided the way to replenish her life was a demonstration to bring Eve to her sense of accountability towards His authority, and not what she assumed to be right in her own eyes. She had to humble herself and let God initiate the healing to her heart that only He could give. Not even Adam could have reinstated her to God's status because he himself was in need of reinstatement.

My dear sisters! Hmmm! I believe God in His wisdom knows that our lives, though affected by sin, can be fully re-established by His grace and love. No amount of hurt, illness, diseases, pain, sufferings, grief, wounds, failures, disappointments, heart-breaks, or downfalls can never ever be too much for God to forgive. The only person who can hinder your forgiveness and failure to forgive others is '*You*'. We are the ones who have to reflect the mind of Christ regardless of the offender and the wrong committed. Our template and model of forgiveness should always bear the imprint of Christ's heart and not what we feel, think or assume. Forgiveness is so sacred, that unless we apply it in any given circumstances where it is needed, we will lose the essence of Christ's sacrifice and disallow our own healing as well as others.

To bring this home to your psyche a little bit clearer, let me help you with a few things to note here as to how much of a medicine forgiveness is to your well being. First of all, forgiveness is the depth of love embedded in the cross, and it is the only antidote for true healing. Forgiveness literally is the key ingredient that connects and sustains healing, to the point where restoration is fulfilled. One cannot find true healing unless forgiveness is initiated. In fact, this act breaks down every barrier that sin seeks to penetrate and makes room for less attachment or association to old wounds. While pain may be a natural effect because of an injury, once forgiveness is applied, it releases the tensions, lessens the burden and takes the weight off, by providing an avenue for freedom. Furthermore, forgiveness brings a person into the acceptance of truth, and with this acceptance, change becomes inevitable. As truth is received, it directs a person towards conviction and this change becomes the stepping stone towards healing.

The principal thing here is that forgiveness goes hand in hand with truth and truth goes hand in hand with change. As a person yields to forgiveness, it then unlocks the door to confrontation and confession, which allows truth to be applied. In fact, forgiveness reveals truth and exposes the nature of sin, to the extent that the heart is no longer willing to subscribe to sin's doings and biddings. To simplify, sin becomes obnoxious to forgiveness, they cannot live in the same place.   Therefore, truth as it is received, becomes the vehicle that transports the ingredients of change to channel one's heart into freedom. As a matter of fact, no doctor can prescribe a much better medication for the heart than what Christ has given to us. Forgiveness truly gives us a healthier way to live.

My friends! Let's embrace God's healing in our hearts and so learn to empty ourselves in His presence; unveiling our deepest secrets, the shut doors of agony, the closets that are filled with unwanted residues, and the years of discomfort in our spirits.   This is not a time for us to hold back and remain complacent; but a time for God to refresh our spirit with His forgiveness so that we can in like manner forgive others their trespasses.   So ladies, go ahead, and face the mirror, face God with all your baggage and let Him heal your heart, your spirit and your mind, restoring you into His love and righteousness.

Chapter 9

'The Enemy's Ploy at Creation'

Amidst the mass and the dreadful plague of sin in the world, you can live above that said sin and rise to a life in Christ that would outshine what the devil intends. You can allow the woman God designed you to be, to come to the forefront and be all He created.

We've journeyed quite a long way so far and I believe that each heart has experienced some type of relief, release, detoxification or ventured into a mode of thinking that has caused a stirring in order to grasp the reality at hand. My dear ladies! God is truly a God who has no limits to His doings and surely man cannot pin Him in a box or chain Him in any way. At this juncture, I am going to take you into a setting that will highlight how the deception at creation presented such a mess for us today. I believe this aspect will be critical since we need to capture the canvas of Eden properly and see the need for God's agenda to take full effect in our lives. It is hard for me to continue and not bring this whole theme of appropriating our womanhood from the context of Eden into perspective, especially, from an angle which many of us fail to perceive, as being one of history's greatest plots by the enemy.

Deeply embedded in this whole drama at the beginning, is a well polished scheme that the enemy crafted and we have managed to fall into his never ending battle of misery. I figured when he challenged Eve's mind towards deception by penetrating her intellect with all sorts of propaganda, he forgot that his intentions would never be able to outweigh God's eternal plan. He was smart enough to have waited until creation was complete to introduce what he thought would have been the right stimulus to annul God's plans. In his efforts to relinquish Eve's mind from God's instruction, he used a bait that Eve had no idea about, since she was not even aware that he once tasted Heaven's bliss.

Sad to say, that although the enemy was skilled and cunning in his ploy to sabotage Eve, he lacked the eternal genius to achieve his end game. You may be wondering what I am referring to here, but though he was successful in one area, his eventual plan was shattered when God visited the garden. Can we view this a little closer? Yes, it is true that sin entered and life was not the same, but I need you to go a bit further with me here ladies. The real issue at hand, was not just the desire of the enemy to deceive and cause Eve a living nightmare; and mind you, his motives were subtle and will always be no matter how much we may try to underestimate him. Capturing Eve's thoughts and swaying her mind from what God directed was just the shadow; but when Eve gave Adam the fruit and he ate of it, there and then was where his deception took full reign. Both parties of God's creation were now experiencing the poisonous spell of the enemy's intellectual deceit.

What both Adam and Eve missed in this whole ordeal was that when the enemy created havoc between them, he just wanted to bring their very nature to a state of decay, by trying to eradicate the very life they were experiencing in God. After all, they were created for His purpose and glory. Their entire beings were now infiltrated with a substance that affected every area of their lives, both physically and spiritually. Up to this very day we are so accustomed to hearing this Genesis story from only one end that I believe what most of us miss is the fact that the enemy was trying to eliminate *'Life or the very breath they breathed- the very spirit of God in man'* from both entities

[111]

of creation. Therefore, he soaked their conscience with a recipe that was masquerade with a deadly intent. Apparently, Eve was the one who became the primary target to succumb to his scheme. But, the real question is, why was he so determined to 'Go Through' Eve?

Here was Eve in a position perhaps without foreknowledge of the enemy and his spiritual twists to mask his influence over her mind. Yet in her opinion, she thought it best to strike back with her own sense of wisdom. Little did she know that the enemy's well esteemed intellect was so powerful to manipulate her very mind. Not that she wasn't perfect, but outside of God, we need to be far more cognizant of our desire to do things our way or through our eyes. For some reason, Eve probably thought it was no big deal to talk back to the serpent and to share the directive she had received from her Creator. But little did she know the trap and downfall she was speedily encountering!

Let me simplify this a bit more. We are quite aware that man was made from the dust which became the natural fiber or fabric in which he resides. And note here, God was the one who breathed into man and so he became a living soul. Man was given a living organism, **'T*he Breath of God in his Being'**, but was still clothed in a natural fabric, that of dust or matter. Now, be mindful to note that the way in which the enemy *(Serpent)* entered the garden was not known either to Adam or Eve. They had no clue about his presence until he actually spoke to Eve. The way the conversation was unveiled demonstrated that Eve really had no idea who this serpent was disguised as. Neither did she think it to be strange. Now, I know that there may be a lot of room for questions, and I'll admit that I cannot give an answer without both of us seeking God's wisdom. Not that I am diluting or depleting the scriptures but there is much room for clarity, in order for us to see the bigger picture. Naturally, the book of Genesis truly offers so much insight that I'm left baffled and speechless as to how this whole drama with creation unfolds. Therefore, I am moved to share this insight with you.

I am sure that many of us who take time to read and meditate on the Word are often refreshed with new revelations and insights that leave us breathless. And for us to understand our errors as God creatures, we must return to the beginning, which opens the door to show us the way back home to God's purposes and plans. In fact, I believe that the enemy's plan was far greater than just seducing, enticing or tempting Eve to disobey God. Apparently, that was the initiation to his complete agenda of which neither Eve nor Adam had any thoughts about.

Look at the way the enemy entered the garden; unaware and unnoticed, waiting for the right moment to set his motives in motion. Of course, it was another cool day and dwelling in the confines of her home was naturally Eve's way of celebrating her environment. After all it was her habitation. Expecting a stranger was not even disturbing her day's proceedings and taking time to say hello was a mannerly habit that everyone should be apt to do. So, she indulged and allowed the serpent the common courtesy of a privileged conversation. Groomed with her politeness, she conversed as the serpent questioned. In spite of the serpent's deceiving intentions, Eve humbled herself to afford the serpent the comfort of enjoying her habitat.

The funny thing is, the serpent maliciously thought it kind to share his generosity by offering a fruit to the host of his day since she was so kind to communicate with him. Instead of eating all by herself, her nature of being equal with Adam encouraged her to share with him; and so he ate. Yet, throughout the conversation, the enemy was not detected by Eve until the fruit was eaten by both persons whom God created. Immediately after partaking of the fruit, God came down for a visit. What was in this fruit that the enemy was able to spoil both Adam and Eve's nature and spirit and cause decay in a way that has left the whole creation in such a dreadful state? How is it that the enemy had such power to influence these two persons; a power that neither of them could have come to grips with or far less prevented from poisoning their natural and spiritual being? Neither of their eyes was opened until both parties ate of the fruit. So what was the enemy's real purpose in making sure that Adam and Eve ate of this fruit? Hmmm!

Interestingly, it was not until they both ate of the fruit that they realized they were naked and ran for cover. Right here we notice that the effect of the fruit targeted both persons and not just one. Why? I find this to be rather interesting as I read and discover the contents in these written pages. Look at it carefully, Eve was the first to eat but her eyes were not yet opened until she gave to Adam and he ate. Then both of their eyes were suddenly opened to the reality that they were naked. So the enemy was not only interested in Eve being baited but more so that the two were caught in his grasp. The funny thing is, Eve was the final entity of God's creation, the very highest level of creation. Now many of you who are reading may wonder if I just had sudden amnesia with that phrase, but to your surprise, the answer is no. If you view how both Adam and Eve were created, you will recognize that Adam had no clue about how Eve was designed, much less created by

God. All he knew was that he awoke, and there was Eve. Soon, after the enemy stepped in with his plan of action. He waited until the finale was set in motion, then he launched his attack.

My mind goes wild right here with all sorts of thoughts, as if we have passed over a crucial component in the devil's tactics that has been maligned for years. Follow me for a minute, ladies. Now the enemy was mindful to be so observant of God's work that he found it pleasing to wait until the work was complete. To him, nothing suited his liking better than to go about his affairs since the platform was rightfully set in motion. Look who he thought best of approaching, the finale of God's creation. Isn't that something to pause and think about for a second? Why did the enemy not go after Adam instead? After all he was made first and surely he was the right person to tackle with such questions, instead of Eve. To me, the enemy was quite clever and he pursued the one who carried an extra bonus from God's design.

Permit me to say here, if there is a man reading this book; please do not feel offended by me making mention of the statement above and ladies be careful not to flaunt yourselves with any sort of heady feeling above the man. This is not a biased motion to have you exercise any wrong concept or ideas above man. Remember, we are not in a battle of the sexes. We are carving a frame from Eden on a canvas that will help both parties of creation to understand how much we have missed the mark. I am sure we have exhausted the whole issue with man versus woman and I am so tired of the faulty picture hanging over each of our heads. So let's keep our composure here and work together to get the real portrait that I am trying to paint before our eyes.

There is no telling as to what the enemy will do to defile the *'magnum opus' (the Latin term for great work or masterpiece)* of God's handiwork. Scripture shows us that the enemy framed himself as a serpent. What a clever way to secretly present himself. I figure that anyone who knows what a serpent looks like and how well it can camouflage itself will certainly be shocked to your wits end if you suddenly discovered one unaware. You would not believe how beautiful such a creature appears, the thing is you may even be tempted to touch it. This creature is so manipulative that it will fool you with its appearance but internally it carries a deadly weapon that will leave you lifeless in seconds. Furthermore, the serpent is so cruel in intent, that it will juice the very life out of you by wrapping its entire body around you until you are breathless.

Even though the enemy took on such a disguise, his intentions were clearly spelt out. Unfortunately for him, he presented a deceptive trait that left him unsuccessful regarding his aim and purpose to destroy, to this day. To truly grasp this reasoning, you will have to go deeper than usual and see with your spiritual eyes the loathsome and horrendous demise the enemy had plotted. Although Eve disobeyed God's command and violated His principles, the serpent knew exactly what his spell would have caused when Adam and Eve both ate of the fruit he gave. I doubt very much that the enemy would have been satisfied to know that they both sinned and nothing further happened, and that life for Adam and Eve continued the same without his plan taking effect.

To say the least, it was not just about their disobedience but what their action allowed to come into existence and the power that same act of disobedience gave to be used as a ploy by the enemy, to achieve his motive at creation. This means of defiance was the very channel that opened the window for the enemy's deceit, that of sin and death entering mankind's being. And since death was mirrored with God's life, so too creation was infected to the degree that life will always be in competition with death. We can view it like this: God gives life and the enemy infuses it with death, something that infiltrated God's creation to the point where Adam and Eve had no cure for survival on their own. Call me a fanatic, but I believe the enemy was rather hungry for power, so much so that he had to get his hands on God's creation. In other words, he had to sabotage creation for his own good or means since he could not possibly create anything of his own.

What we need to understand is that in every way the enemy will do whatever it takes to grapple with God's power and authority in order to replicate his reputation or illusive status. What the enemy sought to accomplish was exactly what God had done with Adam and Eve. Knowing that he could not create life, he in turn used it for his own good pleasure, so that he could control life at his will. Adam and Eve were encapsulated in such a way, to the point that sin's infection was realized; God's very presence was moved to seek out His creation's interest, since He was the Creator of the living. Here is where the devil's intentions were detected by the very One who created life. The devil wanted nothing more than for life to become his art of creation and so he thought it best to defile those who were created, with the thought that life would be made known to him.

Destroying God's creation, since he could not create, would have been the best option. Little did he know that life was not his design or creativity. To the enemy, the toxin deposited in Adam and Eve was his specialized antidote to taint God's creation but to the enemy's surprise life was not marred except for the physical fabric of man. The spirit of man was still breathing; still an organism that outweighed his well intended plans. Man was living in something he could not understand, something beyond his intellect, something the enemy could not define far less figure out for himself. Instead of seeing fury in God's eyes regarding Eve's response to his deception, he saw mercy. They were all cursed but his mind blew out of control when he saw mankind given another habitation. Yes! He had the advantage to ruin their lives and to make life a living hell on earth but for some odd reason he failed in his pursuits.

What he thought would have worked for him, suddenly took a turn that only allowed him to be infuriated. God, after realizing that life was interfered with, took immediate action and knowing that He alone had the absolute power to create; fought for his creation rather than affording the enemy the advantage over His creation. All three subjects were cast out of Eden but God kept something from their knowledge *(The tree of life)* that they never knew. This tree of life was so preserved that no matter what the enemy tried, life could never be nullified or duplicated. I guess the enemy thought that by attacking Eve, *the mother of all living*, the one responsible for birthing, the carrier of life, the receptor of the seed from man, the last creation, life would have been subject to his rule. Certainly, the seed of man cannot produce on its own, so if the receptor of the seed is abolished, what would be the outcome of the seed in man? Obviously he cannot produce on his own since he is the projector. Are you seeing the picture here ladies? Hmmm! I'm seeing here that the enemy really figured that his intentions would have worked perfectly and by cunning *'Woman'* he would eventually have power to manipulate creation. Oh boy! I cannot begin to imagine if he had succeeded what would be the outcome of our status today.

Oh what a tragedy that would have been! This is something that causes me to really wonder about man at times, about how much they take us for granted. Neither of us can live on our own without each other, hence the reason why the enemy sought to destroy both entities of creation so that he could have annulled the very life God gave us. We were both made in God's image and likeness and this fraction of God's creativity is centrally teamed in *His Spirit* and not in man's ideals. Imagine if the enemy could have annulled the oneness through God's Spirit in us, that joining where we are called one, what would have happened? Just think for a minute if he had the power to eradicate the potential to be life in us, what would have happened? My goodness! We would be no good for ourselves.

The fruit the enemy gave to Eve had the ability to kill, steal and destroy but God in all His wisdom made the earliest provision which was planted right there in the garden, *the tree of life.* The irony about the enemy's error is that, destroying life was his ultimate aim in the game, but his power to incapacitate this said life, had to be conferred upon the very giver of life and not the creation that came from life. His futile attempt, though it left a scar on the material part of man, was insufficient to combat the creator's ability to create. Moreover, the very spirit of man holds the essence of something the enemy will never be able to liquidate.

Up to this point in history, the schemes of the enemy to eradicate life apart from God's design are no different *(Check 1 John 2:16).* The only real way he can do

[119]

so without question, is by a person subjecting their own will to him. Take a good look at the world, our homes, families, marriages, nations, communities and every aspect of life, traces can be found where life, in one way or the other, is sought after in order to be defeated. This outrageous diabolical demise of the enemy is even noticed in the science of mankind's research to transform life according to their own knowledge and ideologies. How foolish of us to think that we can manipulate life in whatever fashion or design based on our own initiatives through the art of science, when in fact we're using the very resources that were created by God. Absurd! Isn't it? Nevertheless, God, through our life span over the ages, preserves in us this same aspect of life that the enemy is still seeking to destroy. We fail to see that the enemy is still seeking to understand or come to terms with the very breath we breathe and how he can replicate life for his own good. In fact, if we are not mindful to let our lives be governed by the creator, we will face the consequences of the enemy's ploy, because in no way can we give life to ourselves.

Ladies, the crucial aspect of this life in us is indeed our spiritual inheritance. We do have the strength through God's mercy to regain this life no matter where it is or was broken. What the devil sought to accomplish through Adam and Eve's disobedience was a life that he could have coined as his own and in so doing he caused us to have a defect in our original design relationship with God. Man and woman bore a stain in their very nature that has for so many years tarnished our outlook from the creator's original model of life to what we as human beings have proposed today. Therefore, having lacked the desire to yield ourselves back to His order, we are now suffering as the enemy desires. Instead of redirecting our lives to God's intents, we are seen battling and fighting against each other rather than living in harmony as *One*. We have gone so far from the Creator's plan that we are now taking matters into our own hands and creating more chaos for our lives.

Seldom do we see men and women bearing the imprint of God's heart in their lives, far less to the original order for living. Girlfriends, we have truly lost sight of God's kingdom, value and worth, but I am sure God's heart is still open to help us be converted and conform to His ways of living. The devil may have done the worst to abort God's plan and purpose for creation but we still have life from the Creator that the enemy cannot defeat in us as long as we are a part of God's kingdom. Listen ladies, the life we have in Christ is far greater than what the enemy presents before us daily and instead of taking the cheap way out, God is simply saying to us. Return to Eden! Our womanhood is still an entity of His creation and deep in the core of our beings, each of us has the ability to rise and become the woman He designed.

The enemy's ploy in creation will always bear marks and scars on the material fabric of mankind. However, what we need to understand is that his motives and intentions to succeed over God's creation does not have the power to permeate the very Spirit of God in us. Take into consideration how the Creator went so far as sending His own Son to reconcile us back to the heart of Himself, despite how much the devil tarnished our lives by sin. And still he did not win the battle over lives. We are seriously infected with sin, and the toxins on the internal parts of mankind have an antidote that the enemy will always wrestle against, all because he desires worship from mankind and acknowledgement as God.

Sad, but I have to admit that there are many who have allowed themselves to be influenced by the *'tricks and trade'* of the enemy's game. It pains me to see just how his deception has infiltrated man's heart to the point of death. The only way for us to be redeemed from such bondage is through the blood that Jesus Christ sacrificed for us. I cannot totally cast off the enemy's ploy as null and void. He has mastered the art of infection so much so, that if we fail to see Christ as our ultimatum, life would be left in his grasp.

Therefore, although life is God's rightful originality, we cannot close our eyes to the fact that the enemy has poisoned our living with a disease we cannot exterminate for ourselves. We must go back to God, to Eden and seek to live as God's original designs. This is the place that the enemy is seeking so hard to block us from reentering. He succeeded in causing us to be banished from Eden but it is not impossible for us to return and be redefined as God's creation.

Jesus Christ is our map and guide. He is our gateway, our channel, our advocate, our mediator, our stream of hope, our eternal epistle and inheritance. It is in Him we are able to withstand the enemy with the power to become and be all God ever intended. In this life stream, is our hope of glory, our very expressed epitome of life. Therefore, for us to ever experience life apart from the enemy's intoxicated poison, we must find our pathway back to God's heart. Therein is where life cannot be defeated.

Ladies! I believe, God, who is so gracious in His mercies have provided beyond our means of excuse and no matter how much this world will try to suffocate our livelihood in Christ; the enemy cannot win over us unless we avail that power to him. Eve may have been the conduit for sin's entrance but God made it possible for us to be reconciled. I am positive that His power in you is more than able to propel you with the faith to overcome. The road may be tough and the enemy may keep pressing at your heels, but I am persuaded that the God in you is able to complete what he started in you through his work on Calvary.

Amidst the mass and the dreadful plague of sin in the world, you can live above that said sin and rise to a life in Christ that would outshine what the devil intends. You can allow the woman God designed you to be, to come to the forefront and be all He created. No more holding back, because the enemy has been defeated and is defeated eternally. Rise on the wings of dawn and stop giving room to the enemy to reduce your life to something that will only reflect sin. You are worth a prize that no one can pay. I believe the very God of this universe is waiting to show you just how to walk and be the woman He has called you to be from the inception of creation. Do not let the plot of the enemy seal your life with decay. Get up and start living!!

Eve lived in spite of the curse, Adam lived in spite of the curse and life exists in spite of the curse. Earth is still in effect, more so, God's plan is still in effect. He has extended salvation through His Son to all of humanity and I believe this is your opportunity to step into destiny, purposeful living; to step up to success and to become the woman you have longed to see exist. Life is yours if you wish to go past the pains; the agony of sin found in every area of your life at present, new life is available, life that will never be the same again. Stop living in the shadows, the dungeons, the dens, the closets, the prisons, come taste and see that God is good and that He can make you whole, a woman beyond your dreams.

Chapter 10

'The Thought of 'Woman'

God created a unique entity of creation and one that is rightfully and equally matched to man, without any sort of bias or prejudice. If any is found, we are the ones who put them there, not God.

Ladies! I believe we are entering a chapter that is going to really tickle your mind. Particularly, this title is one that will introduce us into an area that will cause us to capture how our nature and design as women ought to be modeled precisely as God instituted. This is where our value and worth take on the reflection of the image we need to display, embody and where our dignity is mirrored beyond man's conception and imagination. I believe, we have settled for and compromised our beings to just what men think and propose, so much so, that we haven't truly tapped into the aristocratic wealth of our womanhood. We are worth no less than man in spite of our physical differences and functions but let me assure you that there is no partiality to our creation.

God created a unique entity of creation and one that is rightfully and equally matched to man, without any sort of bias or prejudice. If any is found, we are the ones who put them there, not God. I know a lot of men may wring their hands and get all egocentric on me here, but permit me to say that God's intention over His creation are in no way what we deem them to be. I doubt it very much that we have grasped the full context of His purposes and plans. What we have as God's agenda on the earth, especially, in the church is so farfetched and drawn out from what God desires. We are so caught up with all the dominating ideals and the heady nature of our own pursuits that I believe God sometimes wishes for us to just sit down, be quiet and listen instead of ranting and raving about what we hardly ever stop to fully understand. Outside of His deity and mind, we're lost as to the ultimate eternal creation of male and female, and will fail miserably in manifesting His order in the fullness thereof.

We often claim to understand God, but the way we treat each other, and the way men treat women at times, disgusts the very heart of God. Tell me, where in the Word of God have you ever heard that God closed the mouth of a woman and sealed her nature from being what He intended her to be and become? If I am to take a close look at our cultures today, we seriously have a cleanup campaign to conduct on the part of women. While it may be vice versa, the sad outlook is deplorable on the woman's side. I assume James Brown had a glimpse of reality, when he penned the song, *"It's a man's world"* since the voices of women all over the globe seemed so silent and unimportant that man thought it best to seek dominance for all sorts of reasons.

What happened to the woman God created to reign in equal companionship with man over and on the earth? Was the woman in *'Me'* so unimportant that God had to think twice before He gave me to man? Or was I so inferior that my being only matched the scraps that earth refused? Many of you may sit and wonder why am I sounding so harsh or hard but the truth is, when we peruse history, it's heartrending to even unfold some of our cultures and the way women are treated. Up to date, women are still seen as some sort of object rather than an equal being created by God with divine purpose for the kingdom of God. Men still have their conscience so engrossed with the whole concept of dominance and rule, as if to say women will never become anything better than who they perceive them to be. The appalling psychological twist is so conceited that history has covered the versions of reality that we scarcely stop to ever acknowledge or address.

To embark on putting an end to this whole fiasco and ongoing dilemma; we need to harness a mindset that sees things from a God perspective and not just from man's knowledge or wisdom. In fact, it is only in this century that women all over the globe have taken such an initiative to stand up at the forefront for who they are far more than any other century throughout history. And I believe it is high time that men see women for who they truly are in Christ, rather than what the average mind dictates through cultural suppositions and propositions.

I believe we are in a time where each and every single human being on earth needs to take a stand and reenact the scope of God's perception for our lives, rather than allowing our differences to divide and malign our worth as God creatures. The damage at creation has vastly infused our conscience and the only way we can regain any sort of balance is by reconciling our hearts and minds into God's primary intention in Genesis. What we fail to understand is the whole idea of the enemy's desire to ravish our tripartite beings *(Body, Soul & Spirit)* from prospering in and through God. Remember at creation God breathed into man and he became a living **'Soul'** which means that this aspect of life encapsulates and engineers the very foundation of our existence. Albeit the enemy's greatest aspiration is to kill this *'life breathing connection'* in us. Are you truly getting what I am saying here?

To explain further, just so that we can get this into our minds, the *'Soul'* is that physical embodiment of a person, that moral and emotional, actuating cause of an individual's life. This is a physical principle wired in the human body, the inner or internal man, that moral compass side of us. It is a composite of matter, that part of us where our intellect, will, mind and emotions exist, that part which expresses us on a conscientious level. So you can just imagine if the enemy had the power to create this part of us, what the likely results would be today? In other words, he is seeking to do whatever it takes to make sure that this part of us is polluted or liquidated on every degree. I think the picture is painted quite clearly, right here for you. Therefore, my question to you is this, are you going to sit there and allow the enemy to walk in your life and have this *'Soul'* of yours freely? Or are you going to get up and embrace the life God has afforded you through His Son, in order for you to attain the eternal destiny designed with him?

Forgive me, but I can't imagine you'll just let the enemy bulldoze you out of salvation's plan and neglect the investment of Christ blood on the cross. More so to think that you'll refuse to even give any thought or the least consideration to the end of your life on earth. Hmmm! I cannot imagine that we will blatantly choose to miss heaven's bliss for the enemy's illusional bait. It would be a total shame on our part not to understand that life comes from God and it belongs to Him. I am pleading with you right now with all my heart; do not take the bait that the enemy is offering you. He cannot give you life regardless of what attractive promises or possessions he is offering you. Do not sell out to him because your soul is far too priceless.

Now that I have helped you to understand the sole target that the enemy is seeking and how we need to readdress our mindset as women, let me take you to one principle that I have come to understand. In Genesis Chapter 2 when God caused Adam to fall asleep in order to form woman, He took something very interesting out of Adam, one of his ribs. This is the part that excites me and which reveals something amazing. If you notice or count the number of ribs existing in the human body, you will find that there are two pairs of twelve which equals twenty four ribs, of which both men and women have existing in their bodies. No one has more than the other; it is the same twenty four ribs in each person. Notice carefully that the Bible did not say Eve had an extra rib more than Adam or vice versa. It simply states that God took a rib from Adam, closed up his flesh and formed woman *(verse 21).*

What is most striking to me here, is the way God Himself operated as the surgeon in this whole formation. In fact, not even Adam knew what was happening. This rib always perplexes my mind and I would often ask the question, What was so important about this rib that God chose to use it to form a woman? My answer is, it was simply a representation of **the joining of man and woman, that knitted connection or harmonizing effect within the flesh, that unifying combination which holds the form of woman in the flesh.** I am sure you would have heard the familiar notion, *"Woman came out of man"* which was stated by Adam in verse 22. There is no need to fight the issue. Be careful not to think of any misleading ideas here because only a rib was removed from one of his sides, and God removed it. Let's examine this closer, if you take a rib from someone's side, a void will be there, a space is created and a part of that person's body will be missing. But note here that the Bible did not say either Adam or Eve lacked a rib or knew how each other was created or formed by God. They were simply introduced after their creation by God Himself. In fact, they had no idea about their natural or spiritual form at creation, which means that God did not reveal how either man or woman was created for each other in the garden. Creation was never explained or given any script or manual to male or female. The life or breath theory to creation was within the divinity of the Creator alone.

Another key thought to this is the way in which God introduced man and woman together. He simply brought the woman to man or presented her to him, no questions asked and Adam graciously accepted this human form as part of himself. Without any fuss or fight, he accepted her as part of creation, a joint entity, a unique being just like him. Adam went on to even give her the name *'Woman'* because he recognized that this being was of his same likeness, spirit, form and physical fiber. The only difference was their sex, male and female, but he welcomed her as a spirit being, formed into this original texture as a counterpart of his nature. He did not despise her or reject her as a human; he embraced this being as an equal part of creation.

Adam never shouted for Eve to be taken away from creation. He never asked God to leave him alone in his own world. He never casted off Eve much less turned his back and walked away, refusing her after God brought her to him. What I like about Adam here, is that he took Eve as God gave her to him and called her, *'Woman'*. He understood her importance as a being just like himself and shared Eden as their habitat with no thought of not expecting her to be herself as she was created. He didn't limit her potential, undermine her creativity, reduce her femininity, disregard her as an equal part of his life, nor stop her from representing God in a feminine or human form. He did absolutely nothing to hinder Eve's human and divine capacity from functioning and operating as a fully oriented independent woman or robbed her of her wholeness, much less her identity as a woman. Adam simply respected Eve in all her splendor as a woman and vice versa, not even her value and worth were compromised. She was given the liberty to live in the full context as a woman in just the same way as he lived as the man. Neither Adam nor Eve sought to complicate their lives from what God created them to be in Eden.

Again, I will ask this humble question, where did we go wrong or miss the mark with male and female original formation as God intended for us to be? Why are women so devalued and overlooked on earth today and not seen through God's eyes as they were created to be? I am mindful here not to give women a head push against men, but to bring us back into form. However, we need to begin to reform our thinking and align it instead with what God's original plan for mankind was, rather than continuing in this vein where we keep on missing the mark about each other's value and purpose on earth. Enough has been plastered all over the globe in all kinds of context, content and variations, about the way women have failed. And I believe such thoughts have crippled many women from rising up to become the kingdom natured beings that God designed to function as His created on earth.

I have been in many positions to hear of some of the coined phrases heralded about us women and even men as well. To our great surprise, we're the ones (Male & Female) who do the bashing of each other, the ones who degrade and discredit our creation less than God's intent.

Surely! If you haven't noticed, it's not the animals, the mountains or trees echoing any degradation and exploitation of male and female, but male and females themselves. By all means this makes absolutely no sense to me, since we are responsible for where we are and how we've treated each other. So please tell me, what's with all this opposition against women in society? And what has caused man to fail in his capacity as the head? Women, we will have to admit we're to be blamed in some sense for where our men are, especially when we refuse to see them as men in their rightful capacity, under the authority of God.

Ladies! I am not against the whole idea of us having the opportunity to excel and do exploits, but what bothers me is when we step out of line, out of God's order and force ourselves into the positions where men belong. Yes! I can hear the shouts of those who would say, *"So what happens when things don't work out at home, or when we're hurt by men, or when they fail to function, what should we do?"* Ladies, let us not put up a useless fight here! As I said before, we are all responsible but the truth is men belong where God placed them and so do we. If we can only get this principle right, then all the fuss and fight will cease. We will have the freedom just like Adam and Eve to excel in our varying capacities and be able to maximize and have full dominion over the earth.

I cannot in any way propose that we wage war over men's heads; it's totally silly to do such a thing. What we need to do as women is to learn to appropriate our lives as God ordained. We have suffered long enough from being women in the original esteem of creation. So why waste more energy on what does not qualify us, on what does not propel our identity in truth, our leadership in the equal estate of men, on what lessens our virtue and dignity? Too many of us have lost our status, character, value, worth, essence and context of divine order, and are still availing ourselves like free vegetables on the market for the enemy to purchase free of charge. We have buried our heads in less than who God says we are and have suffocated our potential from taking that full awakening into existence. Our children, homes, families, businesses, communities and every other aspect of life depends on our identity to take form; to account for the human race in one way or the other. How long will we delay and then, eventually self-destruct? Our very divine nature is crying out on the inside of us to tap into the heart of God and be the woman He has called us to be.

We do not need to stifle our thoughts anymore, and paralyze our mindsets from rising to the challenge to be God oriented women for real. I can imagine many of us have been branded enough, locked up, enslaved, imprisoned, trapped, barricaded, held in prisons, shut out from being heard, wounded and the list goes on and on. But the truth is, God is calling us back into formation, back to Eden, back to that place where our lives can reflect His image and likeness, His destiny, His sovereign will, His *'modus operandi'* rather than seeing us helpless and without hope for a better world. Women, we no longer need to feed ourselves with all these negative vibrations and lifeless statements that have no power to keep us back from becoming true women of the universe.

In my own life, at one point I used to believe what many had spoken into my life since they had some idea or knowledge about who I was. I swallowed the lies, the opinions of many that I would never amount to anything since my life took such a slant during my youth. Actually, it was easy to feel that way since in my mind I was already leaning to that end. My own mother's words haunted me most, in spite of trying so hard at times to please her. It seemed at one point that I was living just what everyone said about me. Negativity killed my life, my passion, dreams and thoughts of ever thinking that I could become anything good. For many years I went through life all alone, silently thinking to myself, why should I bother since no one believed in me and expected nothing out of me. Although I pushed myself, I was only able to achieve very little, with no real big ambitions as my backing. I settled for what other people's thoughts and words said I was, rather than coming to grips with who God says I am.

It was not until I entered Bible College in the year 2000 that I began to see that all these thoughts were hindrances from my aspiration to be the woman God says I could become. In fact, to my surprise, I excelled far better than when I was in secondary school. My life took a completely different turn, yes, in the direction God orchestrated it to be. And of course I had to dispel the negativity and realign my life with God's will but it was no run up the mill task. In Spite of it all, I endured and pursued to be the woman God says I am. Today, there is not a better feeling I am enjoying than just being and celebrating the woman in me. What I am trying to help you see here ladies, is that God is the One who made you, designed you as you are, created the nature you are living in, filled you to capacity to function according to His plans and purposes. He created you in His image and likeness, called you by name, placed His Spirit upon and in you, fashioned you into the texture and context you reside in. He fitted you into the unique and priceless feminine qualified entity equal to man and ordained you to live out your livelihood as a woman on earth. Why allow anyone or anything; even the enemy, the opportunity to stop you from fulfilling this call upon your life? In my opinion, the only person stopping yourself is *You*.

God was wise enough to think of you, having realized that Adam on his own could not complete his mission on earth. He knew that this complimentary partner had to furnish His idea of creation and in order for Adam to enjoy Eden in full, presenting woman to him was the ultimate and perfect combination of His will. God never devalued your being. It was He who afforded you the advantage, the right to stand next to man, the right to live in Him as a woman and the opportunity to rise in His power to be all you can be in every area of life on earth. My question is, "Why limit the power of God in you?" Women let us arise, let us begin to take back our humble positions and allow the universe to be infused with true women of the Kingdom of God. Let's rise and build our lives with every measure of divine sanctioning and prosperity. Take the limits off! Rise and let the woman in you live!

Chapter 11

'The 'Oneness' Context'

Oneness is at the heart of God no matter how we may try to ignore it. And for us to begin to see what Eden truly represents and means to God, oneness will have to be the streamline of operation.

The only person who thought of you and decided to let you have a taste or an experience of life was God, not man and surely not the enemy. As a matter of fact, if men were honest they would begin to repent for some of the very things they have done to some of us women here on earth. Make no bones about it! I can see their mouths open ready to defend themselves and claim that the same goes for women. Men, I am not disagreeing with you at all but I simply said, if you were honest. In being honest, you will realize that we will create a better approach to dealing and handling our differences, instead of holding a position that's questionable. So why fight, huh, tell me? I think if we strive to fit our mindsets into the heart of God, then all of what we have been battling against may very well have a turning point. And then, living in harmony would surely be possible.

Our mindsets have been the central theme or battle ground for decades, since we somehow believe that trying to *'Rule'* over each would solve God's mathematical equation. While Eve was responsible for sin's entrance, Adam was no less culpable of opening the door to the whole issue. Oh yes, he could have said no to Eve when the fruit was presented to him, but funny enough, he never asked a question much less inquired where the fruit came from and who had given it to her. Mind you, I am not saying that trust wasn't broken here men, but the whole situation will keep getting worse if we stay in the mood of playing *'Cat and Mouse'*. It doesn't make one ounce of sense, since both parties fell for the trick of the trade. Whether we run or choose to take a side, we will always be at *'Log ah heads'* with each other in this scenario. So, why waste energy when we can utilize our commonsense and try starting from Genesis again.

What tickles our emotions so much is the little word called *'Rule'*. This word has many meanings that even though we may attempt to master it, the likelihood is that we may very well miss functioning as required, especially from the English definition. When God gave man the command to rule over woman *(Gen. 3:15b)*, it was never on the basis of superiority, egocentrism, forced submission, dominance, inferiority, undermining her value, or any such negative connotation that diminishes or lower her divinity on the surface of humanity's pages today. Take a good look at Genesis chapter 3 regarding the curse handed down to Adam and Eve in verses 16-17. Notice precisely what God said to Eve in the latter part of the verse 15. Clearly it's written there, *"Your **desire** shall be for your husband and he shall **rule** over you."* Even Adam had an equal admonition, *"because you have **heeded** the voice of your wife."* I find this quite insightful, don't you as well?

The interesting theory and practical insight here are the words highlighted, and the key part they played in God's rebuke and pronouncement of judgment upon their lives. While Eve was the one through whom the act of sin entered into the world, she had to face the consequence of her actions as well as Adam. Eve allowed the enemy to dismantle that essence of worship in her spirit, that belonged to God and caused an eternal separation. She allowed God's glory or divine connection to be touched by the enemy, that part of her which ought to keep her spirit intact with God. Because of this said act, she had to face the reality of God's judgment regardless of the difficulties involved. Adam, on the other hand, having listened to her, suffered the same fate. As a result of this, Eve is now placed in a position where Adam is entrusted with the responsibility to provide the covering that she needs to remain under the act of worship that God requires. Inadvertently, Adam was also given the task on his shoulder to maintain this position on both levels, physically and spiritually, all because he listened to Eve rather than honouring God's command. Therefore, the responsibility endorsed by God was of greater weight than what they both fully enjoyed in Eden. What Adam and Eve failed to realize was that they both dishonoured the Creator as their ultimate *life stream of worship*. Now they would have to face each other in a new way in order to keep God's initial plan for reverence, through a medium that they would have to work at and work together, to maintain this connection.

In other words, Adam and Eve would now have to serve each other in a physical context since they both destroyed their spiritual status in Eden. They were clothed in a material *(flesh or human nature)* that would have to bear the result of the curse and would have to be the garment they now resided in on earth. Yet God was careful to restore them in Him since they would need His **'Life Connection'** for survival on earth, especially because of the enemy's continual attempts to permeate their lives with sin. To put the picture a little clearer, Eve was now required to serve her husband and to let him be the central protector over her life. On the other hand, Adam had to strive in every way to keep a balance on both sides, working to keep Eve in place or position and making sure that work was produced from his hands for survival on earth. My world! What a trade off on both ends here. No wonder we are having such a hard time to even get close to a sense of unity among a man and a woman because they are always in competition.

Ladies! *'Rule'* as it was given to man does not mean violation in our books, authority without wisdom, and leadership without service or disrespect. God was wise enough to allow man to act as a covering in His place since woman dismantled such a covering over her life and involved man in the process. Men please wake up! You have been afforded an opportunity to represent the veil *(covering)* of God over a woman, not with the notion to be the God of her life. Please let us not confuse our thinking in this regard. **Rule** in essence *simply means that you are responsible for keeping the woman in her place or position where God is concerned, keeping her heart in place where the worship of God is required, leading her and keeping her covered under His protection, having the authority to govern her heart in the nature of worship unto God, having the leadership role to steer her direction and to help maintain her integrity and loyalty to God.*

It is also a voluntary act of submission on the woman's part to a man, respecting him as the one in authority, standing by his side as a compatible partner, availing her heart to serve him in order for God to have full worship out of the TWO as One. It's never with any indication that the woman should be treated as a second class floor mat or should be a slave. Nor should she be held in bondage and treated in the manner we are seeing today. No wonder why women scream aloud when they are imprisoned like this! No wonder why we have lost sight of what God intended at the beginning and how free

[139]

Adam and Eve were in their own skins without all of these restrictions and commands. No wonder God is still seeking for us to get it right because we have been fighting against each other for so long, instead of understanding the need to work as *ONE*.

I can see why women are failing to submit and men are faced with such a hard time of gaining their place in life, all because we have failed to work together as God commanded us. If anyone wishes to argue this case, I think taking a good look at Ephesians Chapter 5:22-33 will clarify this even more. So why are we still out of line with the *Oneness* God is looking for in order to demonstrate His heart in us? How long do we intend to let the enemy rape our lives from being restored back to God's divine order? Christ became the way for us to be reconciled and it is high time we begin to appropriate His order as He desires. We are without excuse regardless of what we may think and if you would be so kind, take a good look at the foundation of family life today, especially, in the church. It is the one place I know that has the highest rate of divorce in society and its unit is under severe attack; it is in the most serious state of destruction. Why? Men and women have failed miserably in representing God's order of creation.

My dear ladies! We are in some serious waters and the longer we take to bring our lives back to order the longer we will continue to suffer defeat by the hands of the enemy since he was the one who plotted our defeat eons of years ago. How can we win against the enemy much less stand in our own will and shut God out of the picture and expect a great applause at the end? There is no way we will ever see victory here. I commend those ladies who have made a turning point in their lives to reflect God's standard, even those who are single and choose to live for

God rather than exploiting their own free will ignorantly. I also applaud the men who choose to do the same and even those who are standing in their homes, holding the fort and affording God His respectful rulership in their lives and families. Both ends of the coin must be recognized here, not just one side. I implore those who have set their minds according to the desires of their heart *(without God in the picture)* to take a reality check and start aligning themselves in order. Anything outside of this would only create disaster.

Oneness is at the heart of God no matter how we may try to ignore it. And for us to begin to see what Eden truly represents and means to God, oneness will have to be the streamline of operation. Women please understand, even those who may not yet be in a relationship with Jesus Christ or in a marriage, God desires worship in all sense of the term and in no way is He ever going to compromise for your sake. He knew Adam and Eve fell out of line but the one thing He was mindful of doing was restoring them with His covering. God knew both of them could not have survived on earth without that defensive armour against the enemy's diabolical plans to destroy the life He implanted in them. Women do not go around thinking that you do not need men to help you or to stand with you. You'll be fooling yourselves big time, or let me say to the men right now, stop helping all the ladies and let's see how they'll survive. Oh! I can just imagine what chaos we'll be in, far more than what is present before us today.

The fact that God made Adam and Eve, should alert your mind that He knew what they were capable of and when they were unified what they could achieve. Remember, they were God's creation and that God himself breathed His life into them. The whole idea should excite your spirit a bit. This means that they are unstoppable with God and not even the enemy can deny them from reaching their full potential on earth. I love the fact that God used His creation to defeat the plans of the enemy just when he thought he had it all made *(Gen. 3:15)*. It is imperative, therefore, for us to understand that we do not have to accept and live in the arms of the enemy's courts. He has nothing over us especially when we operate as *ONE*.

Isn't it intriguing how people can come together when they are responsible and assigned to a task? For example, on playing a field, do you see how a football or baseball team stays focused, plans together, strategizes and works as a unit to complete their task? That alone should spell out the very nature of oneness in us. Furthermore, let me use this analogy that I shared with a friend of mine recently, while going through this same account in Genesis to help you understand how God is so concerned and is pleading with us to become one. Notice, when God made Adam He created him from the dust of the ground and when He formed Eve He used a rib. Now I need you to see this clearly, so please work with me here ladies. Adam was made, single-*One*, Eve was made single-*One*, and God was *ONE*. To paint this clearer, when God decided to create Eve He used *One*-single rib from Adam, nothing less, nothing more. If I am to take a man and woman and add them as God combined, I will still get *ONE* *(Gen. 2:24)*.

Based on the idea that God intended to form **'Oneness'** in His creation, to represent Himself in the triune concept- *Father, Son & Spirit*, He knew it would hold an eternal imprint through their *"Image & Likeness"*. Mathematically, it would be coined something like this, *Man + Woman (rib) = One, which reflects God in essence,*

[142]

Father + Son + Holy Spirit = One. I can imagine some of your faces going, hmmm! Wondering how I came up with this thought but the truth is it helps me see even more why God is indeed our ultimate source of life. If I go back to Genesis it will still bring me to a place of awe at how much God availed to us a life beyond our wildest imagination. Before sin entered, Adam and Eve were in full ecstasy with God. They were naked, and unashamed before God, not lacking in self esteem or respect, far less to be afraid of who they were created to be as male and female. Ladies! I think we really need to absorb this, and begin to allow God the place He deserves in our lives. It is time for us to stop running and looking in the wrong direction, to stop thinking that we cannot live in Eden or as close to it as possible. If God was so mindful to cover Eve under the umbrella of Adam after she sinned, why do you think He is not mindful to cover you in like manner?

I think what many of us are afraid of is actually what we will turn out to be in full, if we give God the opportunity to reign in our lives. So often, we only speak of the bad that we are literally afraid to see ourselves clean and pure before Him. We are even afraid, to the point where we remain in our sins and hug them, nurse them, cuddle them, and leave ourselves in the enemy's arms. Seeing ourselves in Christ anew will only scare us, because we think we are not deserving of it. Ladies! God loves us beyond measure and He has done the restorative work on Calvary for you and me. Although we messed up big time, He is still there ready and willing to receive us with open arms, so that we can have the chance to experience Eden again in our lives. Yes! Right now. He wants you to be one with Him in every area of your life, regardless to if you lost a husband, may not be married, have been left abandoned, have prostituted yourself for years, have been sexually

[143]

disoriented, backslidden out of Church for years, whatever the case, God is the restorer.

There is no limitation hindering you from becoming the woman He determined you to be, not even by man or all that we see promoted in our eyes. He has placed His image and likeness in you. Surely, He is the One who can mold you right back into that same *original, or gamic, authentic kingdom centered, divine design, comparable, unique frame, beautified nature and class of a woman He created you to be.* Why settle for less? Why refuse yourself the one opportunity that your heart has been craving for all your life? Why sit in the seat of defeat and discomfort, torment and pain, when all God wishes for you to have is freedom to be the woman He made you to be? His desire for oneness is for us to understand that His mind towards us will always reflect His heart, that relationship where man *(woman)* and God are *One*.

I cannot begin to tell you what this simple revelation has done to my own heart. To be honest, I no longer constrain my thoughts or life from thinking that I cannot be all of *'Me'* as a woman in God. The beauty about this is when one's life is re-established in God through His Son. It's an amazing adventure to discover how the Holy Spirit can move in your life, to be set free from all these bondages that we have set up and allowed others to imprison us, all our lives. The freedom I now have is unexplainable, just to know that I am in God's order is a wonderful and extraordinary feeling. I am able to be all that I can be as a woman in Him. You may sit and say, but Sheldene it's easy for you and you do not understand. But let me say this to you ladies, whom the Son has set free is truly free indeed *(John 8:36)*. Your freedom to live as the woman God intends is right at your disposal; you either

[144]

take advantage of it or leave it freely to the enemy of your soul. The choice is yours!

Why not make the decision to fully embrace God as your Father? Why not allow Him to replenish your life back to order, back to that oneness with His heart, back to that place where you can fully have the power to become all He intends, under His wings of love and care, under His covering, under His authority? Ladies! God is calling us back to Eden right now in this season. He is sending a message to our hearts in this period and that is for us to get in our positions and to give back men their rightful place, no more fighting, no more **'Tug of war'**, no more screaming and shouting, but for us to see Him as the One who alone has the sovereign will and power to appropriate our lives as He desires. He is calling you back to Eden. Come home!

Chapter 12

'Lifting the Standard'

We need to rise and become the women God called us to be and to represent Him in every scope of our world. It is time to bring back Eden in full view; the kingdom of God in and through us on the earth.

Wow! What a journey we've had. I can perceive most of you beginning to shake yourselves and tapping into your conscience and spirit, trying to consult with truth, while looking for ways to deal with the content of your heart before God. There is no need to frustrate yourself on that note. God has already availed His Son Jesus Christ to us. His blood is more than enough to cleanse, purify, sanctify and surely His Holy Spirit will work in us wherever we are and regardless of our present status. God is no respecter of persons and neither is He too far that He cannot reach you right where you are. My friend, He is just the one who can make you over, anew and whole. This can be possible only if you will open your heart to Him.

Remember, the mirror that you are facing is just an open view for you to see *'You'*, the real you, deep down on the inside. It causes you to face yourself and to look closer than before, allowing that person to search for the marks they would have missed before. The mirror is transparent and will only reveal you, no one else, and most importantly it will cause you to face the truth. Actually, my mention of the mirror at the beginning was for you to take a stand and to face *'You'* through the eyes of Christ, not just the physical side of you, but the spiritual. Now that I have done that, I need you to align yourself with His grace and mercy in order for you to find the missing pieces of the jigsaw puzzle you have been trying to fit for so long. To be honest, the only way it is going to be fixed, fitted correctly and precisely is when God becomes involved in your life again. No two ways about it!

This is the time and season I strongly and sincerely believe that God is trying desperately to get women's attention, to awaken their conscience and to have them return to Eden, as a designer's original. He is so mindful of us that He made the preparation for us to be reconciled to Him, through His Son, Jesus Christ. Let me open your eyes to something here, my friends, go back to Eden for a minute. Notice that when God made Adam and Eve everything that they would ever need was right before them, even His very presence. They were given dominion over the earth, which means that they were in total control over their habitation and they had God as their ultimate source or reservoir *(Gen. 1:26-28)*. Adam and Eve were God's offspring and He did not even restrict them from enjoying their habitation, except for the command not to eat from the tree of good and evil *(Gen. 2: 17)*. Adam and Eve had absolutely everything at their disposal, not one thing was missing or lacking. They were blessed beyond measure! Provision was made to full capacity and God's presence was their absolute shield. Wow!

My goodness! I think I have to breathe here for a minute. What an awesome God! Can you picture what the enemy of our souls wants us to miss out on big time? All of what God intends for us to have, *Everything.* But I thank God for assuring us that this same provision has been availed to us once again through His Son, Jesus Christ. In spite of having to live on earth in a vest that is suited for us, a garment that has been poisoned by sin's nature and condition, of the enemy haunting our souls to death; God in

His mercy has re-established us to inherit this same measure of abundance, even today. He is still willing and able to redeem us to our first home, *Eden*.

Ladies! What are we waiting for, what is really holding us back from capturing this said opportunity in our lives, right now? Your past life as I mentioned earlier, is just a sub-total of you, not the complete you. The complete you, is in Jesus Christ. Your image and likeness is in His Spirit, that life breathing connection on the inside of your being, that spiritual nature which is able to propel you to access His love and grace to become the woman He intends. Kindly remember, that Eve did not allow her womanhood to be defiled and neither did she step out from being the woman God created her to be on the earth. She lived as a woman in full, in spite of sinning against God.

I can name many women from the Bible who stood as real, authentic, genuine and full natured women in God; Mary, Martha, Elizabeth, Esther, Ruth, Abigail, Deborah, Hannah, Rebekah, Anna, Sarah, Jochebed, Priscilla, Naomi, Lois and the list goes on. These are women who made a difference and understood that God created them to function and operate as He designed them to be, without reservations. These are women who moved beyond the norms, cultures, male chauvinism, educational stigmas, stereotyping, social injustice, prejudice, political correctness, sabotage, slander, psychological traumas, mockery, blackmail, religiosity, pride, egocentrism, traditions, sexism, and were determined to leave their print on the map of history for us to know and challenge our own sense of responsibility on earth. Therefore, why should you limit yourself from leaving your legacy on earth?

Women! It is high time for us to raise the standard of our living. It is time for us to get it right, to be the mothers, wives, leaders, educators, politicians, engineers, social advocates, governmental representatives, business owners, real estate agents, intellectual tenants and God oriented worshippers in this universe. We need to lift ourselves from all these chains that have been planted on our feet for so long. We need to rise and become the women God called us to be and to represent Him in every sphere of the world. It is time to bring back Eden in full view; *the kingdom of God in and through us on the earth.* I am thankful that God has given me the privilege to stir your hearts into this ideal state of exchange for a type of unprecedented change on earth, and to open your minds to see how He desires this evolution and revolution to capture our hearts.

God is thinking of us so much that He coined one essential chapter in the Bible to influence and affect us to understand the type or kind of woman we can become when we abide in Him. No greater portrait has been drawn than that which is written in Proverbs Chapter 31. The articulation of wisdom that is clearly spelled out in this chapter should reenact a deep desire in each of us to strive to become such a woman. This woman excelled in her life as a woman, not being afraid to accomplish, to achieve, to lead, to be a wife, a mother, a provider. She is one who is extremely blessed, knows how to bless others as they serve, and who stewards everything in her possession. One who seeks God early, one who invests, one who teaches her children well, one who loves her husband, one who uses her hands to work, one who dispenses wisdom, one who understands, one who nurtures, one who influences positively. She is one who masters and governs well, one who was not idle, one who comprehended her status in full, one who surpassed the average mind, who knows her place and identifies with nothing less than what her divinity affirms. She also didn't limit herself to inferiority or stifle her femininity, or devalued her grace, much less misaligned herself from what God created her to be and become. She mastered her womanhood and did not even lose her identity or integrity, she simply knew who she was, *A Whole Woman.*

I wish every woman on the planet could get a glimpse of this in full to see that what society has impacted us with is so farfetched from what God knows we can be. Oh! How I wish for us to rise and stop defeating our nature as women. My heart aches to see women living under such bondage and chains. It pains me to see so many women, even in our churches, suffering because they are still so far from becoming all that God made them to be. I am glad that I've been liberated. My hope at the end of this book is to see nothing less for you. In fact, this book has been a journey or should I say a birthing process of this same experience; since I was crippled in my own world, thinking that I would never become or be the woman God wanted me to be. Just to go through was hard enough and I must admit that I would have fallen so many times before I saw the light. I started this book in 2006 while working as the registrar at my former college and to see the birth of the woman I now am, God alone deserves the praise.

Ladies! Trust me; God can do the same through you. He can liberate you and His arms are open to invite you back into the heart of Eden. Why not give Him the privilege of leading you to be the woman you can be in full measure on the earth? The woman in you is crying to come out. Rise to the challenge. Do not be afraid, for surely you can be a woman of virtue and God in all His mercies will afford the woman in you to shine as pure and refined gold.

Please, I'm imploring you ladies. Do not give the enemy room to destroy the 'Woman In You', the woman God took time to create, fashion, construct, and design for His glory. You are too important to the heart of God to be seen as a waste in the enemy's courts. Ladies! Surely God values you more than that. It is in Him your value, virtue and integrity are revealed, not by the approval or addictions of men. Rise up Oh Woman and live! WOW - **Women Of Wealth.** Come home to Eden!

Pray this prayer with me,

"Heavenly Father I open my life to you, I give you my all, with holding nothing from you. Let your Son, Jesus Christ fill my life anew, let your Holy Spirit cleanse me through His blood and create in me a clean heart. Father, make me the woman you designed me to be. Take off the limitations, the past hurts and pains, the misery that would have haunted me for years. Oh Father! Forgive me of every sin that I ever committed. I rebuke the hands of the enemy from destroying my womanhood. Cause me now to rise in your newness of life. Let your Holy Spirit overshadow me and give me the grace to be a better person, a better mother, a better wife, a better handmaid of your kingdom, a woman of worth, wisdom, wealth, value and virtue. Father, help me to live out this woman in me, that which was formed in your image and likeness and show me how to walk in you daily. Strengthen me Oh Lord, I pray. In the name of Jesus Christ, your Son, Amen."

I trust that as you pray this simple prayer, that the restorative power of Jesus Christ will resound in your being and cause you to rise and become all you can be in this universe, a woman full of God's divine nature, unstoppable and without limitations.   Rise and live! Eden is your home and surely the woman in *'You and Me'* will soar on eagle's wings. Fly, fly high and beyond because you are a woman of divine destiny.   May God help you to be all He has called you to be on the earth as it is, in heaven.

Chapter 13

'The New Creation Woman'

*She is the crescendo, the final, astonishing work of God.
Woman! In one last flourish creation comes to a finish with
Eve. She is the Master's finishing touch.. (John Eldredge)*

First off, it was never my intent to add another chapter to
this book nor to expand your imagination in the womb of
revelation. Nonetheless, it is a necessary indulgence of
grace and love. And might I add that this is a bonus treat,
especially for the women of recent years who invested and
exposed my life into some of the most advantageous
experiences. Permit me to also state that maturity has
given me a kind of evolution in the mind of Christ that I am
bound to advocate and graduate the consciousness of
women into globally. Ladies! We're in the 21st century and
this generation is no longer interested in the pious form of
religiosity or the likelihood of false impressions that
nullifies our kingdom character. So, as my ink flows on
the content of these pages, it is with great passion that I
articulate as needed.

Truth be told, I was advised to consider doing this
revised edition, and as I contemplated, I didn't wish to
rehearse history or step into my closet of unpleasant
memories. But, when I began, I realized that the woman I
am now vastly obliterates the least version or resemblance
to that picture, and it dawned on me that there's a more
valid reason to let my cup be poured out, once again. It is
not for the sake of notoriety, but sobriety has a way of
opening the soul to see its true nature, especially on the side
of nakedness, purity and authenticity. And upon this merit,
I am humbled to enter a principle and theory that women

must understand if she is to be universally and divinely structured for reformation, redemption, revolution and restoration.

While I penned the former narration on the backbone of Eve's story from creation and mirrored my childhood experiences through its lens, I want to transition you into a revelatory scope. Reason being, we've given the idea that a woman in her formed position and posture holds a limited tense to creation. And this is due to the one dimensional view or concept of knowledge from past theological findings, yet I dare say that intelligence to this end is not confined by a tent perspective, but can only be further investigated by one's inquest and desire to go beyond the norm. Being one who is prone to revelation, I've come to recognize that 66 books and its script ends on the basis of writing, but remains potent in the spirit of the same. In other words, ladies 66 books have a conclusion, but the *Mind and Spirit of God does NOT.* Therefore my challenge in this chapter places a type of peculiar demand on you, yes woman, *YOU.* And it is as simple as this, can you *LIVE* in the essence of your creation, in the life breathing entity of eternity without submitting to the confines of man's limitations and a lesser revelation of you? Read on…

Now, I've gone through all the explanatory stages in the last 12 chapters, and I don't wish to bore you with repetition. What I am going to do is take your mind into a revelatory reservoir and I want you to journey with me. That's it!! Nothing spookie or ill intended. Ladies, I am only mindful to open your eyes and mind to see, know and grow beyond the veil of man's perception and the intellectual confines that systematically projects your womanhood to a lesser estate of your divinity. For the record!! You are *MORE* than what man tells or teaches, and it's sad that our male counterpart is engrossed in some of the most hideous acts of injustice toward the true advocation of women. My God and My Lord!! No wonder God formed the woman outside of the knowledge of man, yes, while he SLEPT. *(Gen. 2:21)*

My emphasis above is not to lure your mind into any haughty expression that will make man the least subject of interest, but more so to let man understand that his marginal idea or thought of a woman does not hold the eternal script or full comprehension to her creation. In fact, history may be too painful to rehearse and the cultural confines are no less of a theatrical scapegoat. Yet, we're engrossed in a war that is not merely entwined by *"A Man Vs A Woman"* but what lives in the belly of systematic control and the matrix of the world's ideologies. Let me assure you *WOMAN,* the genius mind of God that formed you is not equated with man's lower concepts, and it will do you well to start appreciating your divine nature as the sole premise to effect and manifest the truth of who you are. Woman! Yes you, the one who is reading these pages, these very words right now, you are the end of God's mind, and the genesis of His thoughts. You may read this and wonder what in the name of Jesus I just said... Uhmmm!! I can see you reading that statement twice, shaking your head and trying to capture my meaning. Oh my word!!

Ok Ladies!! Before you close the book and run off, at least I'll suggest you get a cup of fresh coffee and sit with me. Let's get to the meat of what I mean and end this book with a common interest- *To Help Women Live In Their New Creation Realm.* Agreed? Ok, then let's proceed calmly please. The main reason why I use Eve as my mirror or as a reflection of my divinity is earnestly due to a type of realization that we haven't deeply considered or give attention to study more keenly. When God formed Eve, Adam distinctly stated that she is *"The mother of all living"* *(Gen. 3:20)* and I believe we've missed a key component in what lives in the womb of this statement. Eve comes from the Hebrew word- *Chavah/Havah*- to breathe, *Chayah*- to live or to give life. Traditionally, Eve also means life or living. Being the first woman, Eve held something quite sacred in her womb, and that is the nature of life or the divine breeding ground to produce, give birth, or to let *LIFE* continue in its organic order. Everything in Eve's nature or *WOMB* speaks of nothing less than *LIFE* and can produce nothing less. She was the carrier of **LIFE,** or the mother who all living things had the ability to be ***produced through, in, from, within, inside, or outside of.*** Life was her mainstream portal.

Ladies!! Right here, you may just want to take a deep breath, inhale and stop for a moment. Nothing on earth or in earth is void of *life- **the very Breath Of God.*** Do you understand even more now why the enemy went to Eve and not Adam? He had to go to the one who was the carrier or divine portal of *LIFE.* Woman! What is in your womb or the depth of your creation, the life breathing portal in you that you're yet to realize? What's within the living entity of your breath you've never stopped to discover or even pay attention too? What have you given to man or to the enemy that has dominated your life from experiencing the true spring of eternity in you? Eve literally is an expression of the living well to all of humanity. God was not unwise when He formed her and gave her to man because He knew that this said creation would be the one to give life to all mankind. Without her, life on earth stops!!

So, frankly speaking, there is no way a man can determine the last stance or position of a woman. If men could only accept the truth and that is, they cannot live or ever have dominion on earth or even live in the full expression of God's glory in Christ outside of the woman. Any man who defies the idea of a woman being equal to a man disregards the very theory of creation in its rightful estate. The whole earth is an expression of the *WOMAN-WOMB*, the very bride of Christ is an expression of the Woman, every molecule on your breath speaks of the nature of a Woman, and for anything to have a replication of life, the Woman/Female cannot be exempted out of the equation. Woman! I am simply saying, you are *MORE* to being a living organism and a continuation to humanity than you may ever believe. The institutionalized sculpture we've encountered and have been confined by throughout history is no longer able to keep your lives captive or bound from this truth. I believe this is an era where women will come forth and defy some of the most hideous acts of injustice across the globe. Yes! This time is echoing a clarion call unlike no other, and the earth is groaning beyond to see the depth of this revelation.

Furthermore, as I let this penship flow, woman please know that you are one of the greatest phenomena and enigma of creation. And every part of you holds a vault to life and its ability to produce what eternity embodies. So do not think for one second that Eve's nature as a woman was void of God's answer to redeeming life or was outside of His intent to give life. In fact, Eve's anatomy details the living ground or breathing ground for the transaction of life. Without her, life in any physical or replicate expression, any form that gives the very fiber or DNA to existence would not be possible. Remember, God is Spirit, and anything He needs done on earth, a host/human is required. Therefore, God knew exactly why He used Eve as life's portal on earth, and the need for humanity in all its essence of living has to function in divine order.

From today, as you read the final pages of this book, I want you to take a look at your creation as a **Woman,** look deep within the consciousness of you. Do not let anything bombard your mind from having this moment with you. Stop! And Think… Because there are some elements to the knowledge you're living in that does not befit the absolute truth about you. The database system within you, that illustrates your life may very well be in need of recalibration and renewing. If you are going to live in the new creation of you, yes, on the merit of Christ salvation *(2 Cor. 5:17)* you will have to consider what's been affecting your creation from having an organic and original experience? You will have to take an inventory into *YOU-Spiritually, Physically, Mentally, Emotionally, Socially and Environmentally.* Lady! There's no escaping of this reality, and by all means, your creation holds the power to thrust you into the epicenter of your body, soul and spirit so you can excavate all the unwanted elements that have been preventing you from living in the full divine nature of *You.*

You have the ability to live in the *New Creation* of Christ. Yes! Everything He did on earth and by virtue of His crucifixion granted you the privilege to experience the reality of heaven on earth. It is due to the *New Creation* in Him that you can live in the fullness and abundance of life, that which obliterates and annihilates what was of the former construct of you, what sin depicted, what your past painted, what history narrated, what your environment shaped you into, what enveloped you into the woman you're living in and told you that is all there is to you. Yes!

The lies you've swallowed over the years, and succumb your mind to live in, and here you are at this age of your existence still longing to be liberated, free and breathing in a space that lets life speak the *TRUTH* of you. When will you stop to understand that God never put a *LID* on your creation as a woman? He never put a stop button to your existence/life, why, because you are the continuum of life on earth.

Therefore, you, by being a *New Creation* in Christ can experience the bliss, harmony, unity, beauty and grace that can dispel all the erroneous script of what you once lived. Remember, it is Christ in you, the hope of glory that is at work, not the mere account of man. You're embodied in the essence of life, eternity, the breath chamber of existence and there is no stopping to what can be produced out of you, as a created woman, by the Creator. You are *The New Creation Woman!!* The woman who holds an eternal vault of life, who has the power, dominion and authority to fill the earth, over and over again. No man can stop you from living in this divine experience, but *YOU.* The question is, will you let the dictates of man's theological premise be the definitive factor that draws the last word and sword over you? Or will you challenge yourself to step into a better and more liberating definition to the divine *TRUTH* of who you really are, on earth?

If I am to be honest, I have grown immensely over the years, and having delved deeper into 66 books, I will never let my creation, as a woman, be defined by the theories of man, and the world's knowledge base systems. While I am grateful for the educational merits and virtues, and would not act illusional in my school of learning, I am more mindful to search deeper, especially from *Within- The Spirit Of God In Me.* Through this space of refreshing, I

[159]

have experienced some of the most amazing and fulfilling encounters that only God knows He deserves to be glorified in today. My life as a woman, a leader, a kingdom advocate and apostolic grace to the Body Of Christ and humanity has transformed in ways I do not have enough room in this book to express. I never thought my past had the ability to see the power of salvation and the grace to be defined in the *New Creation* of Christ. And I am loving every moment of it, in full. Woman! As I close this book, I implore of you, please give yourself the opportunity to rise, because the **Woman In You- The New Creation Woman**, is more than a gift to humanity; you are literally a *Life Breathing Entity Of Eternity, On Earth, As It Is, In Heaven.* Now, **Go Live and Be LIFE** to earth!! Shalom.

Printed in Great Britain
by Amazon

39601696R00089